Through
BLOOD
and FIRE

Through
BLOOD
and FIRE

The Life of General William Booth

TREVOR YAXLEY
with CAROLYN VANDERWAL

Foreword by JOHN DAWSON • Preface by WINKEY PRATNEY

CASTLE PUBLISHING
AUCKLAND
NEW ZEALAND

Through BLOOD and FIRE
Published by Castle Publishing Ltd
PO Box 68-800 Newton,
Auckland, New Zealand
Phone: +64-9-378 4052
Fax: +64-9-376 3855

ISBN 0-9582124-4-9

Cover design and layout by MORLEY DESIGN GROUP
Printed in New Zealand by Wentforth Print

Illustrations and photography courtesy of
New Zealand Salvation Army Archives

Scripture taken from the
Holy Bible, New International Version,
© 1973, 1978, 1984 International Bible Society.
Used by permission of Zondervan Bible Publishers.
Other Scriptures taken from the
Holy Bible, King James Version.

For more information:
T.F. & J.B. YAXLEY
PO Box 303 Warkworth,
North Auckland, New Zealand

CONTENTS

ACKNOWLEDGEMENTS

Our sincerest love and thanks to Carolyn Vanderwal for her hard work, inspiring faith, and incredible diligence. Her research and editing have made this book an accurate depiction and powerful teaching tool of William Booth's life. Along with her husband Peter, they are an outstanding example of faith outworked, and an immense source of support, encouragement and love to Jan and I.

This book is dedicated firstly to the entire 'team' at Lifeway Ministries Trust Inc. You have laid down your lives for the sake of the gospel in our nation. Your courage and faith inspires me daily.

and

To all those who have, and are, faithfully serving in the Salvation Army. We owe you an enormous debt of gratitude for your inspirational example of sacrificial living and perseverance. Thank you.

and

To the joys of my life, my family; Jan, my soul-mate for the past 34 years, David (now with the Lord), Mark, Rebecca, son-in-law David, and Renee and Shania, who would have to be the most beautiful grandchildren anyone could ask for. You delight my heart.

"Blood and Fire" indeed! Denoting the power of the blood of Christ and the fire of the Holy Spirit, this famous phrase came to hold another meaning for some; heroic workers who shed their own blood when attacked by vicious mobs but refused to compromise their calling. This is a story we need to know.

After preaching on the boardwalk in Atlantic City I was presented with a gift by local Salvationists - a beautifully preserved antique Salvation Army Officer's uniform. It is one of my treasures. It speaks to me. The stiff high collar and radical insignia came to symbolize commitment unto death for those who wore this garment. Just to look at it fills me with reverence for Booth and the pioneers of the Army.

The story of the Army is truly amazing. It has moved me to repent of having a small expectation of God. Booth was an innovator who understood the needs of his generation. He used the latest technologies and broke out of the straightjacket of religious presuppositions about ministry. He employed dynamic women as apostolic leaders and uneducated street people as preachers. Most remarkable, he redeemed the military motif in an era of empires. He used the discipline, commitment and long-term planning venerated by military culture and infused it with new meaning.

Booth's leadership of the Salvation Army reveals a legitimate polarity within the styles of biblical leadership. More directive than democratic, it represented the resurrection of apostolic leadership in a day when pastors subject to committees were prevalent. To this day the Salvation Army is the only major movement within the Body of Christ that expresses the militant personality of our creator. Because of generations of service to the poor and needy, the Salvationists are able to represent the 'Lord of Hosts' without being mistaken for advocates of violence. Imagine if any other movement put on military uniforms? We would probably be roundly condemned in spite of our protestations about the legitimacy of 'an army of love.'

I have personal reasons for recommending this book to you. It was while serving as the Urban Missions director for Youth With a Mission, one of the world's largest mission societies, that I first glimpsed the awesome power of united, dedicated believers in impacting a world-class city. I was reading a classic biography of Booth, *The General Next to God,* on a flight from Changmai to Bangkok and the story of the first generation of the Salvation Army became my inspiration. To me it represents the high water mark of urban missions. It demonstrates city-transforming power that has challenged subsequent generations to match its impact.

I have a deeper debt to the Salvation Army. Many years ago a young woman knelt at the penitent bench in a storefront mission in Cuba Street, Wellington, New Zealand. She was giving her heart to

Jesus. She was my great aunt and through her the grace of God began to pour into my troubled family.

"Make your will, pack your box, kiss your girl, and be ready in a week," Booth once said to a volunteer and I feel similarly commanded by the life and example of 'General' Yaxley every time I have worked on some project with this remarkable man of vision.

Trevor has served us well by using the story of Booth as a way to prophesy to this generation. Well researched and well written, this gripping tale of one of the great heroes of the faith needs to be read by Christian leaders and new believers alike. I needed this book. God used it to rekindle my devotion to evangelism and discipleship.

Thank you William Booth. Thank you Jesus.

JOHN DAWSON
Los Angeles, 1999

"On April 9, 1865, Lee met Grant in the parlour of a
private home at Appomattox Court House.
He surrendered his army, bringing to an end
four long years of death and devastation
called the Civil War.
In the same year, a 36 year old Englishman
by the name of William Booth, declared war
on the powers of darkness by founding
the Salvation Army."

PAUL SMITH

Since its humble beginnings last century, the Salvation Army has pioneered its work in over one hundred countries, and their shelters, rescue homes, farm colonies, and emigration bureaus, have done more to reclaim the fallen than any other agency. We might perhaps truthfully say, they are doing more to rescue the fallen than are all other agencies combined. Now here in this book, Booth, long since gone, still speaks.

Why did God use William Booth?

1. Booth Understood And Loved The Poor

When William was only a teenager, his father lost his entire fortune and died wholly destitute. Booth was left behind watching his devoted and godly Methodist mother trying to take care of their family alone, encouraging them all to be good and not give up. Booth grew up in poverty and understood the struggle and suffering of being poor. He knew what poverty could do to someone. The poor were his kind of people, and he knew them and loved them deeply. He once wrote:

> *"The men and women around you are weak. They cannot stand up against their own perverted appetites, the charms of the world or the devices of the devil. God wants to pour the Spirit of power on this helpless crowd. But He wants holy people through*

whom He can convey that strength. He works His miracles by clean people. That is His rule."

2. Booth Understood And Loved Holiness Of Heart And Life

William was not just a man with a radical social mission, but also a man with a radically saving message. The gospel Booth preached was a return to the old paths of righteousness, with a call to entire consecration of heart and life to the Person and purposes of God. It was a God-centred, Divine right-on-your-life based proclamation with the ancient teeth and fire of personal to global transformation built into its platform and preaching. He challenged his people:

> *"The first thing God asks is that we possess the character that He approves. You might say the character that He admires. The very essence of that character is expressed in one word, holiness... no other qualities or abilities can take its place. No learning or knowledge or talking or singing or scheming or any other gift will make up for the absence of this."*

While 'less creed and more deed' is a Salvation Army fundamental, their great foundational doctrines were repentance, faith, and the need for a holy life. To the Army, repentance was not just being sorry for sin, but a real turning away from sin. Faith was not some brief intellectual act, but a real reliance of the soul upon Christ, beginning instantly but continuing through time and eternity.

Holiness Meetings were held every week in Salvation Army mis-

sions around the world to lead Christians into a sanctifying experience. Such holiness for them was not just imputed, but also imparted
by the indwelling Spirit. How else could they hold indoor and open air
meetings every night of the week and two or three times on Sundays,
summer and winter, rain or shine, without the power of the Holy
Spirit? What else could have kept every Salvation Army soldier at his
post seven days a week and taking part if possible in every meeting?

A strenuous life must have supernatural strength. The General realised this, and made sanctification, or the filling of the Spirit, a fundamental Salvation Army doctrine. The Booths built on an apostolic foundation, preaching neglected aspects of God's Word often feared and
avoided by those who sought salvation without a real surrender to the
Person and purpose of God. Booth's original name for his ministry
was the Christian Revival Mission - and revival it was indeed. Mere
legislation and devout moral intention are never enough to bring re-
demption to ruined men and women; only a Gospel of grace, power
and holy abandonment preached in the Holy Spirit, could bring about
real and radical reclamation in the world in which William and his wife
ministered.

3. Booth Cared For Nothing More In The World Than The Souls
   Of Men

Booth's passion for souls is clearly portrayed in the following ex-
cerpt from a sermon entitled The Seven Spirits of God.

> "What is your duty here? Oh have you realised your true busi-
> ness in this region of death? Having eyes, oh that you could see!

Having ears, oh that you could hear! Having hearts, oh that you could feel! What are you going to do with this graveyard? Walk about it in heartless unconcern? Or will you content yourselves with strolling through it, taxing its poor occupants for your living while leaving them quietly in their tombs as hopeless as you found them? Heaven forbid!

God has sent you into this dark valley for nothing less than to raise these doom-struck creatures from the dead. That is your mission. Go and do it again. Go and look at them. Go and compassionate them. Go and represent Jesus Christ to them. Go and prophesy to them. Go and believe for them. And then shall bone come to bone, and there shall be a great noise, and a great army shall stand up to live and fight and die for the living God."

Everything Booth called Salvation Army, and all those under his military leadership were geared to one thing; the taking back of the citadel of souls from sin, Satan and the quicksand evils of secular street society. A Salvationist was truly devoted; willing to sacrifice everything - old friends, family ties, wealth, possessions, comfort, security, acceptance, social accomplishment - to see the beachhead established, the spiritual breakthrough made, the citadel won back for God's Kingdom. "Pack your bags, make your will and kiss your girl goodbye," was the word for the new recruit, "You are going to war."

4. Booth Knew What It Was Like To Be Rejected, Persecuted
   And Hated

From the time Booth first preached on the street in Nottingham, he was jeered at, mocked and ridiculed. Throughout the early years of the ministry of the Army, its young soldiers had to dodge missiles of rotten fruit, dead animals and rocks from a crowd that did not appreciate being called out from the deeply entrenched wrong that filled the nation. Salvation Army missionaries and evangelists saw themselves as real soldiers; in town to fight the enemy and win back that, which had been wrongfully taken. Theirs was a war of holy love:

> *"He loves you. He has told you so again and again. He has proved His love by His deeds. Love compels the one entertaining the affection to seek the good of its beloved. He knows that sin is the enemy of your peace, and must mean misery here and here-after. For this reason among others he wants to deliver you from it."*

Salvationists were roped, punched, kicked, spat on, pelted with ship's rockets and burning sulphur, while entire gangs of hundreds, even up to thousands, rallied to stop the little holy band. But they marched into town anyway, covered in slime but not ashamed. Kneeling in the centre of the town they lifted up their battle cry: "Lord Jesus, in Your name we claim this city for God" and then they got up to take it!

5. Booth Was Willing To Risk Everything To See Souls Saved From Sin

Booth was intolerably ahead of his time. Famous Christians opposed him for his disrespectful abandonment of traditional, religious and safe methods of ministry. His Army sang to converted bar tunes; they used outlandish gimmicks and advertising to get people to listen or come to the meetings. They were loud, disturbing and doggedly committed to the cities' highest good. Booth once summed up their position stating:

> *"At a great Christian conference the other day an eminent divine said that the Salvation Army believed in a 'perfect sinner,' but that he believed in a 'perfect Saviour.' This, I contend, was a separation of what God has joined together and which never ought to be put asunder. For glory be to the Father, glory be to the Son, and glory be to the Holy Ghost, the Salvation Army believes, with its Lord, that a perfect Saviour can make a poor sinner into a perfect saint. That is, He can enable him to fulfil His own command, in which He says, 'Be ye therefore perfect even as your Father in heaven is perfect.'"* MATTHEW 5:48

Booth's clothes were baggy, his tired face was baggy and his eyes were baggy, but he preached with such power, conviction and compassion that men who heard him sometimes felt literally pulled up from their seats, lifted up from the crowd, and deposited at the altar of surrender to the living Christ. Above all, William Booth loved Jesus and loved people for Him and it showed:

"But alas, the great multitude are like children; they require to see and hear God revealed before their very eyes in visible and practical form before they will believe. And to reach these crowds, God wants men and women to walk about the world so that those around, believers and unbelievers alike, shall see the form and hear the voice of the Living God; people who shall be so like Him in spirit and life and character as to make crowds feel as though the very shadow of God has crossed their path. Will you be a shadow of God?"

Booth and his holy army visited more countries, spoke more frequently, won more souls for Christ, and rescued more fallen men and women than did any other person in street ministry history.

WINKIE PRATNEY

Could a mariner sit idle if he heard the drowning cry?

Could a doctor sit in comfort

and just let his patients die?

Could a fireman sit idle, let men burn

and give no hand?

Can you sit at ease in Zion with the world

around you DAMNED?

LEONARD RAVENHILL

We want men who are set on soul-saving;

who are not ashamed to let every one know that this

is the one aim and object of their life and that they

make everything secondary to this.

CATHERINE BOOTH

CHAPTER ONE

Hell No!

L ate one evening in 1844, 15-year old William Booth trudged wearily home through the shabby, dimly lit streets of Nottingham, England. The stench of open sewers and the snarl and hiss of marauding cats, mingled with the muffled cries of young children echoing behind cold, stone walls. Booth was well accustomed to the dark oppressive atmosphere of the city streets, yet tonight the sights and sounds compounded upon the strange uneasiness welling up from within. During the last few hours his thoughts and feelings had been deeply provoked by Isaac Marsden, the preacher at a meeting in the Wesleyan Chapel.

"A soul dies every minute!" Marsden had thundered at the somewhat bewildered congregation. The challenging words played over and over in young William's mind, stirring up a torrent of unanswered questions with an urgency he had never before encountered. "I would have given myself to God if my friends Boldie and Will weren't with me," he argued with himself, trying desperately to justify his failure to respond to the preacher's challenge. His breath hung heavily in the cold autumn air, lit-up as it drifted by the occasional gas lamp, a light for drunks stumbling along the dark streets.

As he wound his way through narrow alleys, his troubled heart was suddenly overwhelmed by an incredible sense of his sinfulness. Cold tears trickled down his trembling cheeks and froze on his chin as an urgency to be free from sin's grip rose within him. With his heart pounding relentlessly, the Spirit of God fell upon him bringing immediate conviction and heartfelt repentance. This was the beginning of a new life for Booth. Allowing God to deal with him, he began immediately to bring his life into line with what he knew to be godly.

As a young man, he was a passionate, wilful, and at times an impulsive character. The fiery spirit of the Methodists had struck a chord in his heart that night and he began to attend their meetings with great enthusiasm.

Two years later, as he sat spellbound by revivalist preacher James Caughey, Booth's life was revolutionized, and without hesitation he dedicated himself to the service of God. "I want to be right with God, I want to be right with myself, and I want to spend my life helping others to be right," he stated emphatically as he reflected on his decision to live for God.

From that moment on he was branded with a consuming passion to save the souls of men. The same sense of desperate urgency that had consumed John Wesley almost a century before, now also gripped William Booth. In many ways he began to tread in the footsteps of Wesley, preaching in the open air, his heart beating in unison with the multitudes of poor and weary, who would never darken the doorways of the lavish churches and cathedrals of the day.

Willie, as his young friends nicknamed him, was not one to let the grass grow under his feet. He didn't wait to be given opportunities to preach the message of salvation that burned within his heart. He made them! Creating opportunities was part and parcel of every day for this enthusiastic witness of the gospel.

Standing on a chair or barrel in an alley or on a street corner, he would invite people to attend meetings in a nearby cottage where he would preach a salvation message to any who cared to listen. Booth's natural flair for relating to people enabled him to communicate the gospel message in a way his audience could understand.

His first success came with a preaching venture that found this tall beanpole of a lad in Kid Street with his friend, Will Samson. Expectantly, they positioned themselves on the street edge, outside the home of a notorious drunk, 'Besom Jack.' Their open-air meeting commenced with a hymn that seemed to be appropriate for the occasion. It was from the Methodist songbook:

Outcasts of men, to you I call,

Harlots and publicans and thieves!

He spreads His arms to embrace you all;

Sinners alone, His grace receives:

No need of Him the righteous have,

He came the lost to seek and save.

They had no sooner raised their voices than a large boisterous crowd encircled them. Young 'Willie' was on his chair in an instant. "Friends," he cried, as he dodged a well-aimed over-ripe missile, his large hooknose having a somewhat magnetic appeal to the tomato launching public. "I want to put a few straight questions to your soul," he declared passionately.

At that moment the front door behind him flung open and out stumbled 'Besom Jack,' eyes aflame and heading straight for the preaching duo, shouting abuse and lunging at them while still six feet away.

"Jack, God loves your wife, and so did you once," said William steadily, looking the broom-seller in the eye. Jack stopped in his tracks and immediately became quiet. "Can you remember how much you loved her and cherished her when first you met?" the teenager asked tenderly. Jack nodded, his eyes fixed on the ground. "Well, Jack, God loves you with a love like that, with a love far deeper and greater than that." The hushed crowd strained to catch what the boy-preacher was saying, amazed at the change that had overcome the drunkard. Jack lifted his eyes and blinked sheepishly. "Me?" he asked in wonderment. "Yes, Jack, you," said William as he stood down from the chair and took hold of Jack's arm. Jack's wife recounted the end of this meeting to Mr Eames, the pawnbroker, the following week saying, "And 'e said to 'im, 'Come Jack, just kneel down 'ere and tell the Lord you love 'im too. And ask 'im to forgive yer.' And 'e did! My Jack knelt there in the gutter and 'e's bin a different man ever since; 'e says 'e's a Christian now!"[1]

There was birthed that day in young Booth a heart that beat for souls... for souls... for souls.

As a young man, Booth made a choice. He chose the salvation of men and the extension of the Kingdom of Jesus Christ as the supreme object for which he would live and work. Like Moses he had grown to maturity and *"chosen to forgo the pleasures of this life, preferring to share the oppression, suffer the hardships and bear the shame of the people of God rather than have the fleeting enjoyment of a sinful life."*

This object of salvation, this purpose of the Kingdom, continued to shape and master Booth's thoughts, ambitions and activities through-out his whole life. All that he accomplished was governed by his de-sire to live and work to see salvation come to all men and the King-dom of God extended in the world in which he lived. From the age of 15 William knew what he was about.

Booth's church leadership and close acquaintances soon recognized God's gifting on his life and encouraged him to enter the Methodist ministry. He hesitated over this decision for many months, discouraged against such a step by his poor health and dire lack of finances. Instead he moved to London, working in his pawn-broking trade and expending his spare time and energy in saving souls and preaching as a layman in his local church.

In 1851, Booth's lay preaching in the Wesleyan Methodist church came to an abrupt halt when renewal of his membership was refused due to his sympathy with the Reform movement. The dejected young man felt the sharp sting of rejection as he was stripped of his oversight and the opportunity to preach. He searched for new avenues of ministry, and at one stage seriously considered paying passage to Australia on a convict-laden ship bound for the colony. The chance to "face the storm and the billow, and the tempest's rolling wave, and to preach to the very worst of men, Christ's salvation,"[2] appealed immensely to William's adventurous nature. This was not to be however; God had His own blueprint to fulfill through this love-laden loyalist of calvary's cross.

A wealthy friend, Edward Rabbits the bootmaker, recognised the potential in the fiery young evangelist and came alongside to encourage him through this difficult time. Rabbits not only invited Booth to join with The Reformers but also supplied an income of twenty shillings a week for three months, to enable him to quit work and focus on preaching the gospel. Booth's name was eventually added to The Reformers' preaching plan and soon after he preached his first message in their Binfield Road chapel.

Sitting in the congregation that day was another friend of Edward Rabbits, Catherine Mumford. Rabbits introduced Booth to Catherine and on another occasion invited them both to his home for tea. Their third meeting was at a Good Friday service in 1852. At the conclusion of this meeting, William nervously offered to escort Catherine home from church, as she was feeling unwell.

"That little journey will never be forgotten by either of us," Catherine recalled in later life. "We felt as though we had been made for each other, and that henceforth the current of our lives must flow together."[3]

In less than a month William and Catherine were engaged to be married. Although they spent much of their three-year engagement apart, Catherine was to become, as Norwegian biographer Clara Thue Ebell described, "William's human pillar of fire." The relationship that developed between them was one of mutual sacrifice and submission and of the sweetest love. Catherine was a source of constant encouragement, guidance and inspiration. Together they became a formidable team.

Booth continued to preach whenever the opportunity arose and moved for a time to Spalding to work with The Reformers. In 1854

Catherine persuaded him to return to London to study under Rev. Dr. William Cooke in preparation for the ministry of the Methodist New Connection. Dr Cooke soon recognised that this unique lad was not a student to bury in books and study, rather, he was a passionate revivalist whose unscholarly and unorthodox preaching methods were well received by ordinary people. Booth's mentor was so impressed with him that he arranged for his appointment as minister of the Packington Street Church in London. In addition to his leadership of this church, he also continued to preach in response to invitations, holding revival campaigns all over England. The meetings were a great success. The leadership of the New Connection acknowledged his evangelistic gifting and consented to allow him to serve full-time as an evangelist within their movement.

William and Catherine were married on 16 June 1855, and Catherine immediately joined her husband in revival meetings around England. Her health was very poor and consequently she often had to return home, leaving William to campaign alone. Although the success continued, with thousands making decisions for Christ, the local churches were barely able to cope with the influx of new converts. Negative sentiment toward Booth grew steadily as ministers became frustrated with the disorder and chaos created by the revival meetings. In 1857, the leadership of the New Connection withdrew him from the work he loved and restricted him to Brighouse in Yorkshire, one of their least promising circuits.

Catherine Mumford shortly before
her marriage to young William
Booth, in 1855.

William and Catherine were married on June 16 1885, at Stopwell Green Congregational Church, England.

James Caughey, born 1810, greatly
inspired the ministry of William and
Catherine Booth.

William Booth, captured in a
thoughtful moment.

In 1858, Booth became a fully ordained minister and was shifted to the Gateshead circuit for a period of one year after which it was promised he would be released to evangelistic work again.

During this same year James Caughey returned to England and was back on the revival trail. While William was away, preaching on the circuit, Catherine decided to attend Caughey's meetings in Sheffield. A few days later, Caughey called to visit the Booths at home. His time with them sparked something in Catherine, who began to wonder: If Caughey was free to preach when and where the Spirit led him, why should not her William do the same? [4]

Finally in 1861, Booth appealed to the New Connection Conference to fulfil their pledge and reinstate him to the work of full-time evangelist. Instead he was appointed as Superintendent of the Newcastle Circuit, a large and very tough circuit, which would never allow him the freedom to carry out revival meetings elsewhere in Britain.

So, with Catherine's support and in the face of vigorous opposition, Booth handed in his resignation. His formal connection with the Methodists was over. The movement that had so openly embraced him now firmly closed its doors. Wesleyan and Primitive Methodists across Great Britain forbade the Booths the use of their chapels.

Free from the restraints of circuit work, Booth and Catherine began once more to travel throughout Great Britain, holding evangelistic campaigns and championing the cause of the poor and needy. A very successful series of meetings were conducted in Cornwall resulting in the Booths praising God for the response of over 7,000 people to the Gospel. Their itinerant work continued for four years before they finally moved as a family to London, feeling drawn for the first time to the masses who called the city 'home.'

A powerful sense of destiny rested upon Booth as he strode through the busy Whitechapel slums on his way home one evening in June 1865. The small congregation he had addressed just an hour ago were already forgotten, as the stinking depravity of the East London streets bombarded his senses. As he approached the small crowd that had gathered outside the Blind Beggar pub on Whitechapel Road, he heard the leader of the open-air gospel meeting ask if anyone else would like to speak. Always ready to seize an opportunity to preach, Booth did not hesitate long enough to be asked twice.

With fiery zeal and an authority known only to those who fear the Lord, he scuttled the complacent hearts of his listeners with a directness and compassion few could withstand and even fewer would ever understand. Booth finished his appeal and continued on to the warmth of his Hammersmith home; but the sights and sounds of reality did not leave him.

Within days, the leadership responsible for the street meeting approached him and asked if he would take temporary charge of the work. A series of services were being held in a dilapidated tent on the site of an old Quaker burial ground in East London, a stones-throw from the slums of Whitechapel Road. William Booth had 'found his destiny.'

The way ahead was not easy; the path was strewn with obstacles. The life of an evangelist, especially an evangelist to the poor, was fraught with difficulties. By this stage the Booth household had grown to include six children, with their seventh child due in just five months. The supply of money required to feed, clothe and house this large family was scant. Times were hard.

"We have trusted the Lord once for our support and we can trust him again," Catherine boldly stated as her husband spoke passionately of his desire to stay and work with the poor in East London.[5] Together they chose to forge ahead, with little except a strong conviction from God to sustain them.

Torn apart by the poverty, the drunkenness, the prostitution and disease that characterised the slums of England, and convinced of the power of God to change even the hardest man, Booth strove to win the East-Enders to Christ. It was, as biographer Harold Begbie stated,

"the spectacle of sin and suffering that moved him to give himself to East London. He went out and looked upon the woes of the people both by day and by night. And he could not walk a yard

in those dreadful streets without suffering in heart and in mind.
He heard in all that misery a heartbreaking cry for help. And he
had no rest until he gave himself to the work of rescue. The true
way of relief for any who is conscious of misery of any sort is to
take a hand at fighting it." [6]

The aim of this work in East London was to bring the message of salvation to those the church had failed. The people they aimed to reach were those like the drunken miner who sought out the assistance of a parson. "Read your Bible," was the parson's reply. The man had to confess; he could not read. The parson then suggested he should come to church. When the man explained he had only working clothes, the parson ran out of solutions. Such was the attitude of many image-conscious clergy of the day. Perhaps God might have helped the drunken miner, but his spiritual adviser was powerless to do so.[7]

The limitations and spiritual poverty of the church indelibly coloured the emotions and attitude of this defender of the poor and neglected. Booth was convinced that the gospel message was indeed the power of God for the salvation of all mankind. God had laid on his heart the plight of those the church had written off as not worth reaching. Biographer Richard Collier describes Booth's dedication to the poor in the following account:

"As a teenager, Bramwell Booth never forgot the first time his

Bramwell, Booth's oldest son,
was destined to follow in his father's
footsteps.

Enthusiasm was the hallmark of young and old in the early Salvation Bands.

father led him into an East End pub: the illumination from gas lamps playing eerily on men's inflamed faces, drunken dishevelled women openly suckling tiny children, the reek of gin and shag tobacco and acrid bodies. After a moment, seeing the appalled look on his son's face, William Booth said quietly: 'These are our people. These are the people I want you to live for and bring to Christ.'" [8]

With the conviction that God had called him to bring light into this darkness, Booth began his work in the derelict East End slums. This work was to become the foundation of an organisation expanding in his lifetime to reach the nations of the world. Although this motivator of men possessed remarkable vision, it is not likely he envisaged the future scope of the work he and Catherine began in 1865.

What began as The East London Christian Mission became simply The Christian Mission, as the Booths' work expanded and stretched its boundaries into other areas of suburban London. While the mission continued to grow and develop, its organisational structure grew by necessity but did not seem to add strength to the work. It was soon obviously apparent that the democratic committee style of government that had evolved in the mission was stifling its vision.

Men and women who had committed their lives to this endeavour in order to save souls were being weighed down and held back by endless meetings and discussions. Clear and direct leadership was required from Booth at this critical time of growth and change. After great consideration, the deed poll of the organisation was scrapped and The Christian Mission took on a military style of government under Booth's direct leadership and the officers appointed by him. In 1878, during a leadership meeting, The Christian Mission was declared to be an Army under the superintendence of William Booth. The Salvation Army was born.

In 1879, Booth wrote to his officers:

"We are a salvation people - this is our specialty - getting people saved and keeping them saved, and then getting somebody else saved... Look at this. Clear your vision. Halt, stand still and afresh and more fully apprehend and comprehend your calling. You are to be a worker together with God for the salvation of your fellow men. What is the business of your life? Not merely to save your soul and make yourself meet for Paradise?

Rescue the perishing. There they are all around you everywhere, crowds upon crowds, multitudes. Be skilful. Improve yourself. Study your business. Be self-sacrificing. Remember the Master. What you lose for His sake, and for the sake of the poor souls for whom He died, you shall find again. Stick to it. Having put your hand to the salvation plough, don't look behind you." [9]

A passion for souls governed Booth's life from the moment of his conversion at 15 until his death at the age of 83. The conviction that

ruled his life was the salvation of men and the extension of the Kingdom of God. Reiterating the courageous words of Jesus' apostles to
those who sought to silence them, he staunchly proclaimed, "I cannot
but speak of the things I have seen and heard."

William's mission was clear; his mind was set. He knew what he
was about. As leader of The Salvation Army his battle cry was unmis-
takable: "Go for souls, go for the worst!"

The General in latter years.

Booth encouraged, "...will you leave them as you found them? Heaven forbid! What will you do?...Go, go and compassionate them (show your concern for them). Go, and represent Jesus Christ to them! Go, and prophesy to them! Go, and believe for them! Go!...and a great army shall stand up to live and fight and die for the living God."

It is not said after keeping God's commandments,
but in keeping them there is great reward.
God has linked these two things together, and no man
can separate them - obedience and power.

F. W. ROBERTSON

What can be a more fatal cause of religious declension
than inactivity? Yet there are multitudes...
professing to be Christians who do absolutely nothing
for the salvation of souls.

CATHERINE BOOTH

Are you worried because you find it so hard to believe?
No one should be surprised at the difficulty of faith, if
there is some part of his life where he is consciously
resisting or disobeying the commandment of Jesus.
Do not say you have not got faith. You will not have it
so long as you persist in disobedience.
Your orders are to perform the act of obedience on the
spot. Then you will find yourself in the situation
where faith becomes possible.

DIETRICH BONHOEFFER

CHAPTER TWO

Excessive Obedience

Booth was in his early teens when his father, a tight-fisted builder, faced financial ruin. This sudden change of events in the family business saw the plans for young William's future swing from attending a prestigious school for gentlemen, to being apprenticed to a pawnbroker. His father died soon after his building business collapsed and 'Willie' was bound to the apprenticeship for his family's survival.

These were hard times in England. The gap between rich and poor was widening at an ever-increasing rate. The Industrial Revolution resulted in the loss of jobs for many labourers. These were dark times indeed! For some families, the pawnshop was their only hope to avoid eviction from their shabby dwellings. Through his apprenticeship, young Willie watched first hand the effects of poverty on the lives of people he knew. The incessant clinking of the doorbell and the clomp of dirty worn boots on the damp wooden floor wearied him. His young heart was crushed by the despair etched on the faces of those bringing their most precious possessions to be given only a pittance in return. The haunting sadness in the depth of their eyes added to the picture of hopelessness that gripped and touched his heart. Each day was a reminder that he was among the fortunate ones - at least earning a wage, small though it was.

Soon after his conversion, William began to feel uneasy about working on Sundays. Although the pawnshop officially closed at midnight on Saturday, the staff were often kept working without a break long into the early hours of Sunday morning. Business was booming. Compelled by his conviction that to work on Sunday was against his Christian principles, Booth informed his employer that he would no longer be able to continue work beyond midnight on Saturday.

The proprietor, Mr Eames, was not impressed. His position was clear. "You can work with the rest of us until we shut up shop, or you can leave."

Standing strong in his decision despite the threat of losing his job, Booth quickly discovered his employer was serious. He was fired! For choosing to live by his convictions his only source of income and support was cut off. Joining the hordes of unemployed in Nottingham City, he was faced with scant opportunity of finding work. The streets were packed with slow moving crowds, each person desperately searching for employment, prepared to queue for hours at the slightest glimmer of hope that work may come their way.

William's street walking was short lived, for in a remarkable turn of events God intervened! After just a few days, his employer realised he had lost his most valuable worker. William was reinstated and allowed to finish work on the stroke of midnight each Saturday.

His stouthearted desire to obey God no matter what the cost, evident from the moment of his conversion, became a hallmark of his life and teachings. With the call of God came a healthy fear of the Lord and a strong desire and commitment to obedience.

It was nothing less than this desire to obey God that years later urged Booth to resign from the security of the Gateshead circuit and pursue the call of an evangelist. This was not an easy decision. William and Catherine cut themselves off from a regular income, gave up their right to a roof over their heads and plunged into the uncharted waters of living by faith in God alone. In the early days of their work in the East End slums it was nothing less than their radical commitment to obey God that compelled them to keep going. 'Quit' and 'give up' were phrases foreign to them; dogged determination and passion propelled them forward to meet their destiny. To the Booths, faith and obedience went hand in hand. Their belief in God compelled them to a life of surrender and obedience.

The uncompromising nature of Booth's obedience and commitment was foundational to the style and structure of the organisation that formed around him. Although he did not initially set out to build an army, its militant style developed naturally under his leadership and in the climate of the day.

The nineteenth century was a militant era, impacted by the American Civil War and the Russo-Turkish war. The well-known hymn 'Onward Christian Soldiers' was released to the world in 1865, the year that marked the beginning of the work in East London. These were the glorious days of the great British Empire and the rank structure of Queen Victoria's soldiers was adopted by Booth and his followers.

The militant style developed rapidly and by 1878, when the mission was declared to be The Salvation Army, the name had already woven itself into the fabric of the organisation. As Catherine stated: "...we are an army. We grew into one, and then we found it out, and called ourselves one."[1]

The disciplined structure of the military soon permeated every aspect of this holy Army. Service titles of general, captain, cadet and soldier were adopted. Salvationists began to speak of prayer as 'knee-drill,' of offering envelopes as 'cartridges' which must be 'fired' regularly and their local mission base as the 'corps,' each of which had its own 'citadel' or 'fort.'

Banners and flags were fashioned to reinforce the identity of each corps. The very first Army flag was presented to the Coventry corps in 1878 by Catherine. The flag was red, referring to the saving blood of

An early Salvation Army uniform.

The Army flag that fired passion in Catherine's spirit, displayed outside her birth place, 13 Sturton Road, Ashbourne, Derbyshire.

Christ, bordered in blue as a symbol of purity and a holy life. It was inscribed with the words "Blood and Fire" on a central yellow star to denote the power of the Blood of Christ and the Fire of The Holy Spirit - the two vital elements of the life and work of Salvationists.

Booth encouraged the adoption of a standard uniform that would distinguish the salvation soldiers from their fellow men. The uniforms made a visual statement of commitment and courage and were proudly worn by all.

With the adoption of these military practices came the all too familiar criticism that has been leveled so lavishly at those who choose to forsake all to serve and follow Christ. Booth was touted as being legalistic and exerting too much control over his people. To such critics there was one answer: he could not lead the rapidly growing Salvation Army without such a system. "Had the children of Israel been managed by a committee they would never have crossed the Red Sea," he declared.[2]

He knew the secret of the successful expansion of the movement was at least partly due to the strict structure and management of the troops. Though the rules seemed hard, they ensured 'those who stayed' were aware of the cost, committed to the cause and prepared to do battle in order to triumph over every obstacle and opposition to their passion of spreading the gospel. The Army's volunteer workers were under no misapprehension of the level of commitment required of them. People were never forced to join the Army and comply with the disciplined lifestyle - those who chose to follow God in this way were committed because of their devotion to God and their desire to obey Him, not because of the pressure or persuasion of man.

Although, in the early days, Booth was committed to the work in East London, Catherine was a popular speaker who was frequently invited to speak around the country. Wherever she went, converts were made and this created the need for new mission stations to be opened. Evangelists were sent out to these new areas for a maximum period of six months to see the new converts established in the faith. Booth was determined to prevent any of the stations from becoming a community of settled, contented Christians enjoying their favourite preacher. He wanted only, "Godly go-ahead dare-devils."

"Make your will, pack your box, kiss your girl, be ready in a week," were his terse instructions to one volunteer.[3] The level of commitment was clear - radical obedience was required. Nothing more and certainly nothing less!

Booth always delivered an uncompromising and challenging message. He was a gifted and skilled preacher who held his audience captive whether preaching the gospel or impressing on converts the urgency of taking the gospel to the lost. His son Bramwell describes for us his preaching manner: "... he had, of course - what the humblest of us may manifest - the supreme charm of the public speaker - a sincere and living personality shining through all he said. Sometimes this was more apparent than others. Everything in his talking was striking, but this made it often so winning. He studied carefully to avoid anything unnatural or superior. He learned to allow his human qualities full play - humour, sympathy, frankness - and yet, with all, there was ever a piercing and definite attack on judgment and conscience and heart."[4]

No one could dispute the miraculous power of God that was transforming the lives of the new believers. Meetings would last for many hours, with converts experiencing powerful manifestations of the Holy Spirit. As desperate men and women knelt to confess their sin, they also resolved to live the remainder of their lives in the service of God. They would rise from their knees determined to live life completely surrendered, and totally committed to the One who had saved their soul.

The lengths to which these fresh recruits went to see the gospel preached is an indication of the degree of their commitment, passion and faith. The early Salvationists would do anything to draw a crowd. One man lay silently in the snow every evening for a week. When, by the end of the week, a large and curious crowd had gathered in the market place, the man leapt to his feet and preached his heart out, much to the surprise of his captive, and somewhat stunned onlookers!

Booth's message of radical surrender and total obedience to God attracted great criticism, especially in the early days. To many, his call for no compromise, no holding anything back, no denying God in the small things was too serious and too difficult to obtain. He disregarded their comments, choosing instead to live and preach according to the standard of obedience set out in the Word of God.

The very same issues stood in the way of the nineteenth century Christians as stand in our own way today. When preaching his message of total obedience, Booth encountered those who cried, "the cost is too high, the sacrifice is too great!" Writing on this issue in *The War Cry* January 20, 1881 he stated:

> *"They say plainly that husband and wife, father and mother, brother and sister, houses and lands, friendly circles and business and money and politics and health and big idols and little idols bar the way, and they cannot suffer what it would cost them to come and stand forth before the heavens, having dared to leave and offer all up for the sake of Him who left and offered all for the sake of them."*

Challenging his readers he turned their attention to the martyrs of days past, writing:

> *"O friends, what about these heroic spirits? What about those faces that look at you today through that blinding smoke and those devouring flames? Are there then two standards of service,*

one high and Christ-like for them, and one much lower, made to meet the case of little, lean and cowardly souls? Nay, are there three ways for the feet of those who travel toward eternity? One wide and broad for the wicked, another straight and narrow for martyrs and martyr spirits, and the other a middle middling, sort of silver-slipper path, for those who would have the pearl without the price, the crown without the cross.

No! No! No! Look again at those martyr-men. They stood up there before heaven and earth, and said in the loudest language that can be spoken in this or in any other world, that they gladly gave up, not only friends and kindred, lands and money, and every other earthly treasure, but life itself, which to them, as to everybody else, is far dearer than all else put together, for the truth and love and cause of Jesus Christ." [5]

Booth was convinced the one thing holding back the full blessing of God was the reluctance of people to surrender all to Jesus. He wrote:

"Men and women who will die at their post are the very sort in demand just now in The Salvation Army and elsewhere. They are what the world needs, what we are praying for and what God wants." [6]

His own praying was 'red-hot' fervent, effective and profitable. Heaven was made to feel the force and impact of his petitions. He felt it not too much to ask the same of his officers. 'Like father, like son' was his hearts desire.

In his address to Salvationists for the New Year 1906 The General answered the question "What I should do with my life were I called upon to live it over." He penned:

> *"I should offer my life up, without a moment's hesitation, on the altar of redeeming love. I should place myself - body, soul and spirit - at the feet of Jesus Christ, ready and willing literally to live, suffer, fight and die for Him."* [7]

This passion-filled warrior of the nineteenth century knew the power of the dedicated life; the power that comes as a disciple decides to be entirely committed, thoroughly devoted and totally obedient to the Lord. He lived his days knowing that "a crucified life is an awesome weapon in the hands of a holy God."

Booth's consecration - his unreserved obedience, his total surrender and his intimate devotion to God - was undoubtedly the source and secret of his strength. He knew, "no amount of money, genius, or culture could move the hand of God. Holiness alone energises the soul, the whole man aflame with love, with desire for more faith, more prayer, more zeal, more consecration - this is the secret of power."[8]

Bramwell once questioned his father, curious to know how he could keep on without tiring, despite all the setbacks and difficulties facing The Salvation Army. Booth answered, describing how he had knelt in the chapel in Nottingham at the age of 15 and vowed, "that God should have all there was of William Booth." This was the secret of his strength.

As his daughter Eva was later to add, "That wasn't really his secret - his secret was that he never took it back."[9]

Here is the principle... adapt your measures to the
necessity of the people to whom you minister.
You are to take the Gospel to them in such modes...
and circumstances as will gain for it (the Gospel)
from them a hearing.

CATHERINE BOOTH

Think that day lost whose low descending sun
views from thy hand no noble action done.

JACOB BOBART

The great use of life is to spend it for something
that will outlast it.

CHARLES MAYES

CHAPTER THREE

Innovate & Initiate

I am ready to admit that in the majority of cases the training of women has made her, man's inferior..." Catherine passionately wrote to her fiancé, "but that naturally she is in any respect, except in physical strength and courage, inferior to man I cannot see cause to believe, and I am sure no one can prove it from the Word of God..."[1]

In a little over two months Catherine and William were due to marry. They had been apart for the majority of their three-year engagement as William took charge of a Methodist circuit over one hundred miles from London. Through their passionate letters, written to each other daily, they had grown closer and deeper in unity and love. Catherine's aspirations, dreams and disappointments poured forth from her pen at a rate of up to two thousand words in a single letter.

In this particular letter, Catherine urged William to consider her belief in the equality of men and women in the sight of God. This was radical thinking to most, but for Catherine it was nothing out of the ordinary.

The Victorian woman's world was one of needlework, reading, and polite conversation. There was little or no room made for women in education, medicine, science, politics or the public work of the church. Their lives were given meaning only by relationship with their husband and children. Consequently the woman's world was narrow and restricted, revolving predominantly around home, family and their social circle.

The obvious exception was the plight of the deprived, working class women who had no option but to find employment in factories or as domestic labourers. For the most part, the church of the day merely reinforced society's subjection of women.

As the gifts of God stirred within Catherine, she was compelled to search the Scriptures to find God's heart on this matter. With great excitement she began to realise the equality of women and men in the sight of God. Jesus' teachings and his love and respect for the women he met confirmed her understanding of their place and value. She wrote fervently of her convictions to her beloved, impelling him to consider for himself the role of women in the work of God. She argued, not just for her own benefit, but for the encouragement and release of many gifted women who were stirred by God to be involved in public ministry.

His reply reflected the depth of their relationship and their ability to communicate in a forthright and honest manner with each other. It was clear he needed to give it more thought. He wrote, "I would not stop a woman preaching on any account. I would not encourage one to begin. You should preach if you felt moved thereto; and felt equal to the task. I would not stay you if I had the power to do so. Although I should not like it. I am for the world's salvation; I will quarrel with no means that promises help."[2]

Booth's willingness to consider even the most unorthodox ideas if they might further his one purpose of saving the souls of men, was a key to the success of his mission. He was a man of great vision who was not limited by current thinking or methods.

Although hesitant at first, he became as adamant as Catherine about the equality of men and women before God. The original constitution of the mission reflected this stance, stating: "As is manifest from the Scriptures...that God has recognised and sanctified the labours of godly women in His church, godly women possessing the necessary gifts and qualifications shall be employed as preachers - itinerant or other-wise - and as class leaders, and as such shall have appointments given to them on the preachers plan; and they shall be eligible for any office, and to speak and vote at all official meetings."[3]

In 1860 Catherine also began to preach publicly. She was terrified of public speaking. Many times she had tried, only to back down with incredible nervousness. She struggled even to pray aloud and on one occasion a gathering waited five long minutes for Catherine to open in prayer with a few faltering words.

For years she had written sermon outlines in response to the burning of the Spirit of God within her. Young William had preached using some of these outlines, but Catherine herself was yet to preach her first message. Slowly the breakthrough came. Writing to her husband, following a Methodist prayer meeting she declared with excitement, "And would you believe it, I prayed. I think I shall rise superior to this timidity which has been such a curse."[4]   When the moment finally came, it caught them both by surprise.

During a Sunday morning chapel service in Gateshead in 1860, Catherine was suddenly filled with a compelling urge to speak to the congregation. In her mind she heard a familiar mocking voice, "You will look like a fool and have nothing to say." Recognising its source immediately, she responded, "That's just the point. I have never yet been willing to be a fool for Christ. Now I will be one."

As her husband brought the meeting to a conclusion, she leapt to her feet and strode down the aisle, painfully aware of the murmur that arose from the people. Booth, thinking she was unwell, quickly rushed to her side. "What is it, my dear?" he asked.

"I want to say a word," Catherine replied, now feeling quite nervous. Caught completely by surprise Booth turned to the people and announced, "My wife wishes to speak." Stunned, he sat down.

Catherine opened her heart to the congregation, confessing her own disobedience in the matter of preaching publicly and encouraging all to obey the stirrings of God in their own hearts. With admiration and pride Booth watched as many of the congregation were moved to tears. When Catherine concluded her brief message, he spoke quickly with her and then eagerly exclaimed, "Tonight, my wife will be the preacher."[5]

The news travelled fast. Just 30 minutes later, Ballington and Katie, too young to attend the morning meeting, were dancing around the scullery table following the maid who had just arrived home with the news. Squeals of delight echoed from the kitchen as she sang triumphantly, "The mistress has spoken! The mistress has spoken!"

That evening the chapel was literally packed to the doors. Every available space was filled, with young children squashed together on the floor and window ledges, no one wanting to miss this historic moment. They were not disappointed; Catherine spoke with captivating passion and sincerity. Forthright, fervent and with an incredible ability to cut to the heart of an issue in moments, she wasted no words as she arrested the attention of her listeners.

Within weeks she became renowned as 'The Women Preacher,' a title that stayed with her until she preached her last message 28 years later. Together with her husband, she forged the way ahead for the recognition and respect of the call of God on women. In this regard, The Army led society, challenging and reforming the accepted stand-

Catherine in the 1860's.

Early Salvation Army Band, 1890's.

ards of a culture that opposed the truth and purpose of God. Their actions were founded on the principle of freedom in Christ Jesus - freedom for men and women to be all that God created them to be.

Booth's leadership of The Salvation Army is marked by many more examples of visionary thinking that challenged and changed the status quo. His pioneering spirit seemed to touch every sphere of society from the nature and style of church to the social and welfare structures of many nations across the world.

From the early days, Booth's intent to reach those who were not drawn to the mainline churches influenced the style of Army meetings. Vacant warehouses, dance halls, theatres and even a shed between a stable and a pigsty were used to draw in those who would 'not be seen dead' in a cathedral. Songs were sung in place of hymns, which were considered to be too 'churchy' for the people they were reaching. Messages were delivered with great passion and emotion, as the preachers connected with their listeners, expounding the gospel of Christ and urging those present to respond to God.

General Booth was a keen observer of people and trends, and this, together with his insatiable appetite for change, enabled him to capitalise on new ideas as they sprang to his attention.

He was well ahead of his time with the introduction of popular music into worship services. The instigation of the first Salvation Army

Band was unplanned; it seems it occurred without great thought, happening almost by chance. In 1878, Booth was offered the service of William Fry and his three sons to act as bodyguards during open air work in Salisbury. Almost as an afterthought, they took their brass instruments along with them to the market place. Fry was the choir and orchestra leader of the local Methodist Church. When they offered to play, Booth agreed, much to the horror of the local evangelist who fumed his way through the first two songs - until he noticed the enthusiastic participation of the crowd that gathered. The little group accompanied the singing and the Army's first brass band was born.

What a way to draw a crowd. Tambourines, dustman's bells (dustbin lids), hunting horns and banjos soon accompanied the rowdy 'music' produced by the primitive brass instruments. The lack of musical finesse and the crude instruments were more than compensated for by the contagious enthusiasm and energy of the musicians.

In 1882, a controversial step was taken when the General consented to the adaptation of hit tunes into the Salvation Army repertoire. Although dubious at first, he began to realise the ease with which the 'unchurched' would sing the words of songs with a familiar, popular tune. The way ahead was sealed one evening as he heard a converted sailor leading the singing in a Worcester theatre. The catchy tune seemed familiar to Booth, who loved to sing, and he caught hold of a passing officer inquiring, "That's a fine song. What tune is that?"

The officer shook his head disapprovingly. "General, that's a dreadful tune. Don't you know what it is? That's 'Champagne Charlie Is My Name.'" Booth stood silently for a moment, listening as the congregation finished the song with great gusto. Turning to Bramwell he concluded emphatically, "That's settled it. Why should the devil have all the best tunes?"[6]

The Army embraced their new weapon with great enthusiasm. Within a year of the commencement of the Musical Department, there were 400 Salvation Army Bands pumping out a myriad of hit songs.

Booth's ingenuity and vision found no barriers; the style of the services was in a continual state of change. Every new change was accompanied by a new challenge. These were tackled head on with unique and creative solutions being found and implemented.

When it came to solving problems, the General was never confined to a square box. He encouraged Salvationists to find solutions to the obstacles they faced and supported them in the implementation of new works. No development was seen to be too big or too hard when it came to birthing new strategies to win the lost because, as Booth well knew, 'people last forever.'

With creative foresight and the attitude that believed no problem was too big for God, it is no wonder the Army achieved many 'firsts' in its social and welfare policies. Under Booth's leadership, they pioneered homes for the rehabilitation of prostitutes and ex-prisoners, labour bureaus, sheltered workshops, homes for alcoholics, missing persons' bureaus, cheap accommodation for men and temporary shelters for the homeless.

In India, a Salvationist by the name of Major Frank Maxwell, studied the primitive methods of weaving and concluded they were too time consuming. He invented an automatic two-pedal handloom and then the cam-action auto-loom that was awarded first prize in a local industrial exhibition. His patented auto-loom was soon in use by weavers throughout India, including Mahatma Ghandi's home-industry movement.

In Norway, violent winter storms claimed the lives of many fishermen every year. The Salvation Army decided to help the fishing communities who suffered the brunt of the stormy seas. A lifeboat was custom designed to handle the fiercest conditions, using the best technology and science available to create an 'unsinkable' vessel. In 1900, the lifeboat and her crew were commissioned to save the lives of fishermen along the treacherous coastline. During calmer weather the *Catherine Booth* toured along the fjords, carrying the message of salvation to the fishing villages. Under the command of Captain Emil Ovesen, the crew of the *Catherine Booth* rescued 5000 men in 1772 boats within just 13 years of operation.

Booth encouraged Salvationists to anticipate problems and where possible implement solutions to divert them before they became major disasters. As in everything, he led by example. On May 11, 1891, this entrepreneur opened a match factory.

During the research for his book *In Darkest England and the Way Out*, Booth discovered that over 4000 employees of England's match manufacturers were working under appalling conditions. Women, and children as young as eight, made matchboxes for meagre pay, working 16 hours a day, with no break for meals. Furthermore, the companies were producing 'strike anywhere' matches by dipping the match heads in deadly yellow phosphorous.

The fumes of yellow phosphorous were highly toxic and many of the factory workers complained of severe toothache. The cause of their pain was 'phossy jaw' - rotting of the jawbone due to the toxic yellow phosphorous, that resulted in gangrenous infection and often death.

In response to this discovery, the Army set up its own match factory, producing safety matches tipped with harmless red phosphorous. The factory was airy and well lit, and its 120 workers received fair pay for their work. The policy of higher wages and multiple breaks saw productivity increase. 'Phossy jaw' was eradicated from workers producing Booth's *Lights in Darkest England* matchboxes. News of the good conditions at the factory spread quickly within the industry.

"Worry your oil man, or grocer at least twice a week," was the directive given at every opportunity. The campaigning continued until the local merchants yielded and began to stock the Army's safety matches. Within a year, public pressure had forced match manufacturers in England to conform to the standard of safety set by this industry leader. When the victory was won and match companies adopted the reforms necessary for the health and fair treatment of workers, the Army turned its attention to rectifying other social injustices.

Partnering with a creative God, Booth's work impacted the world. Every opportunity was taken to influence society with godly wisdom and God-given answers. With tireless passion, Booth's example began to impregnate The Salvation Army with a spirit that was prepared to do anything to reach and win souls.

New songs were penned to stir the heart and keep the focus on the Army's purpose. One popular song, invariably sung with impassioned fervour by soldiers and officers alike, gave reinforcement and impetus to the dream.

Oh, the General's dream, that noble scheme,
Gives John Jones work to do;
He'll have a bed and be well fed,
When the General's dream comes true.

For the hungry, starving, homeless wrecks
Abounding everywhere,

This scheme allows that either sex

Shall have a cab-horse fare:

The cab-horse has its work, you'll find,

With food and shelter too;

Man shall no longer be behind,

When the General's dream comes true.

When a cab-horse falls upon the street,

No matter who's to blame,

If carelessly he missed his feet,

They lift him just the same.

The sunken of our fallen race -

A tenth is not a few -

We'll lift them up in any case,

When the General's dream comes true.

For all its innovation and initiative, Booth and his holy Army knew that only Jesus could change the hearts of men. While he encouraged his people to adapt the modes and means by which they related the Gospel to people, he was unyielding when it came to the content of the Gospel message. The message of the cross was never to be compromised. As Booth wrote in 1868, "...we attach little importance to instructing men's minds or arousing their feelings, unless they can be led to that belief in Christ which results in the new creation."[7]

Booth and his holy Army knew that
only Jesus could change the hearts
of men.

Success is not measured by what a man

accomplishes, but by the opposition

he has encountered and the courage

with which he has maintained the struggle

against overwhelming odds.

CHARLES A LINDBERGH

You cannot improve the future

without disturbing the present.

WILLIAM BOOTH

Tribulation is the fruitful parent

of fortitude and faith.

WILLIAM BOOTH

CHAPTER FOUR

CHAPTER FOUR

High Cost

Open-air preaching and parades were part of the heart and soul of The Salvation Army from the outset. Booth quickly discovered that although the working class they were trying to reach would not enter a chapel or a church, they would listen to a speaker who set up on a street corner. Street meetings and parades of Salvationists, complete with the local corps band, became a common sight in the towns and cities across Victorian England. Every parade and open-air meeting would culminate with an indoor service, allowing interested people to hear the gospel in full and have an opportunity to respond, without the distractions that often accompanied the outdoor gatherings.

In the early days, the disruptions were usually caused by a drunk stumbling from the door of the local alehouse accompanied by the boisterous laughter and coarse encouragement of the pub patrons. To the delight of the red-nosed faces peering from the grimy alehouse windows, the drunk would blaspheme and shout obscenities with the intention of embarrassing the female officers dubbed the 'Hallelujah Lasses.' Such harmless interruptions were easily handled with good humour, inordinate amounts of patience and quick thinking. In spite of such opposition Booth forged ahead with the work of the Army.

Expansion of the Army occurred very quickly as new converts eagerly enlisted. Wherever the Booths or other Army evangelists preached, people flocked in. By January 1879, just 14 years after the work began in East London, William and Catherine were overseeing 81 stations staffed by 127 evangelists, with over 1900 voluntary speakers holding 75,000 services a year across England. The sheer volume of administration required for the Army's smooth running was massive. To most the task would have been insurmountable, but William and Catherine were a match for the mountain. Tirelessly, they toiled on.

The majority of the growing numbers of volunteers and evangelists had been converted at meetings run by Army personnel. Stirred by Booth's passion for the souls of men, they too had chosen to sacrifice all in order to bring salvation to those who struggled hopelessly under the oppressive conditions of nineteenth century England.

With no reputation to lose, Salvationists strove to see the Kingdom of God advance in villages and towns across the length and breadth of the land. Morale soared. Divine intervention was commonplace. Anonymous financial gifts would regularly arrive with uncanny timing. A 'barrel full' of these miraculous tales could be purchased from any street storyteller for a farthing. Unswerving, unalterable, unquestion-able trust in the power of the living God catapulted them forward with unequalled momentum. Their detractors stood by bewildered, as week after week this dedicated, determined band advanced the cause of the gospel with unparalleled haste. However, as the work of the Army expanded, the disruptions and attack against their work began to take on a more serious and sinister form.

The early Salvationists were prepared to meet the demands, to bear any cost, to see salvation come to ordinary men and women like them-selves. Their willingness to 'pay the price' was regularly tested to the limit. The reality of the battle was plain to these unsung heroes of the cross. Willingly, they risked their own lives in order to proclaim the timeless message of righteousness, truth and grace.

Preaching on the streets in the early days was like preaching in hell. Teams of Salvationists faced ridicule, scorn and hatred as they openly proclaimed the gospel in the degraded slums. The poor and destitute were strongly atheistic, hating the name of God and fiercely opposing those who spoke of any form of religion.

By 1880, this holy Army was attracting severe opposition. Those who stood to lose most from their success became their most formida-ble enemies. Hotel and brothel owners faced falling profits as their previously thriving businesses began to suffer. The escalating conver-sion rate of many of their most loyal customers was plainly evident. They were conspicuous by their absence!

In 1881, publicans from the village of Basingstoke incited a crowd of young hooligans into attacking the local Salvation Army Corps as they marched in the streets prior to their meetings. The level and frequency of the violence of this angry mob against the Salvationists prompted the detachment of a special force to police the streets in the village. While Basingstoke soon settled down, many other villages across England erupted as violent hordes went on a rampage against the Army.

Booth himself was often found in the thick of the action. In 1882, he joined Sheffield Salvationists in a procession prior to their meeting in the town hall. William and Catherine rode out front in a small carriage, as the Army band led dozens of uniformed Salvationists in the parade. A thousand-strong mob of local hoods called 'The Sheffield Blades' lined the pavements, shouting abuse as the Army passed by. Suddenly, a roar went up and the mob erupted onto the street. Armed with an imaginative array of weapons - from rotting food, dead animals, and great clumps of clay, to rocks and heavy clubs - the angry thugs attacked the procession. The General rose to his feet, missiles flying in all directions. With eyes ablaze he commanded his followers, "Stay near the carriage, stay near the carriage" They did. Pushing on together the battered troop finally found refuge in the safety of their meeting place. Once inside, a great cry went up from the audience at the sight of the Salvationist's blood stained uniforms and the buckled brass instruments. "Now's the time to get your photo taken," Booth half jokingly quipped to his assistants as they stood beside him on the platform.[1]

The violence continued to escalate throughout England. There was little the local police could do. Protection, on the rare occasion it was provided, was definitely a luxury for the Salvationists. On one occasion, 1500 extra officers were placed on duty to shield the Army during its scheduled Sunday parades. However, even this was not enough. The angry mobs continued their violent and unprovoked rampages. William's concern deepened.

The attacks were not confined to the streets and laneways or open-air parades. The rioters stormed the Army Citadels causing many indoor meetings to close due to the uncontrollable chaos. In 1882 alone, sixty buildings used for Salvation Army purposes were all but destroyed by rioting crowds and 669 soldiers were assaulted. It seems no one was exempt from attack, regardless of age or gender. Of these 669 soldiers, 251 were women and 23 were under the age of 15.

Tragically, greater injuries were also inflicted. In Guildford that same year, the wife of the corps officer was kicked to death. A fellow woman soldier was so beaten during the same parade that she also died some days later from the wounds she sustained.

In Whitechapel, East London, Salvation Army lasses were tied together with rope and pelted with live coals. It was not uncommon for parades heading for the evening meetings to be showered with tar and burning sulphur. "Blood and Fire" had become a reality for this army of God, unfortunately not only in the way originally foreseen.

While English law permitted the Army to hold open-air meetings and parades, when they supposedly 'incited violence' amongst local louts and 'caused a disruption of the peace,' local magistrates were instructed to do all in their power to prevent their public work.

Often the magistrates and local police officers were completely unsympathetic toward the Salvationists, many of whom were fined unjustly for petty charges such as 'praying in a public place.' When they refused to pay the fines for unjust charges, the Salvationists were sentenced to jail. This only strengthened their resolve and inflamed their courageous spirits with a heightened fire and passion to see their communities saturated with the gospel.

As the law continued to turn a blind eye to the injustice and violence, the wild mobs grew even more daring. A group of hooligans in Oldham banded together and formed the first of many groups across England and the world under the ominous title of 'The Skeleton Army.' With skull and crossbones emblazoned on their banners and armed with weapons of flour, red ochre and deadly jagged 'brick-bats,' Skeleton Army units attacked Salvationists with renewed vigour.

While Booth, (like William Wallace of Scotland) faced the task of holding his Army together under intense persecution, attack came from other directions as well. He was hated by many influential leaders, especially those who held positions of authority in England's churches. He bore the brunt of great criticism and slander, being labelled an 'indecent charlatan' and even the 'Antichrist!'

Many religious leaders took great offence at his methods of public preaching, and especially at his decision not to include baptism and the sacraments of Holy Communion as essential practices of The Salvation Army. This "Brave Heart" stood firm, refusing to be swayed by public opinion. He was confident the steps he took were divinely directed, radical though they were. Booth was well aware of the tendency for new converts to become dependent on religious forms and to rely on such things as baptism and communion for their spiritual well-being. He knew that if Salvationists were to achieve their purpose they would need to find strength for their service through the Word of God and the empowerment of the Holy Spirit. They would not do anything that might encourage their members to rely on an outward form rather than seek the grace of God personally by faith. Furthermore, as many of his ranks were reformed alcoholics there was little wisdom in suggesting they take the wine of Holy Communion.

This champion of the faith was also criticised and highly resented for his insistence of the equality of men and women in the work of God. The Salvation Army welcomed and encouraged women preachers - a radical move for the Victorian age when a woman's place was clearly defined as being in the home. Booth, encouraged by Catherine's belief that their movement would benefit greatly if women were involved to the same degree as men, firmly planted the equality of men and women before God into the growing structure. "The best men in my Army are the women," he often stated. For much of the Army's history, the women officers out-numbered their male counterparts five to one. Their courage was legendary and stories were published of their remarkable love and sacrifice, even for those who taunted them. One such story was entitled 'The Lass From the Army.'

"She was a Salvation Army lass, and her lot was a hard one. Working from seven in the morning till six o'clock at night, weaving hair-cloth was dull and poorly paid work, but in addition she had to bear the constant and thoughtless gibes of her fellow-workers. One Autumn morning a spark from a bonfire on some adjoining allotment gardens entered an open window, alighted on a heap of loose hair, and the next minute the place was ablaze. A rush for safety of the work-girls followed.

'Is everybody down?' asked the foreman. His question was answered by one of the weavers, who holding up a key, shrieked, 'My God! I locked Lizzie Summers in the 'piece shed' for a joke not a minute ago!' The 'piece shed' was a room to be reached only through the burning building, through which it seemed impossible to make way. Girls and men were standing aghast and helpless, when two figures stumbled through the smoke, which poured from the weaving-room. One was seen to be Lizzie Summers; the other was, for the time, unrecognisable. It was The Salvation Army lass. She had stayed behind, burnt, blistered, and half-suffocated, to batter down the door in order to liberate and save the life of her coarsest-tongued tormentor." [2]

Choosing to ignore his critics and refusing to waste precious time and energy defending the Army against the accusations and slander hurled its way, Booth concentrated on resolving the more important issue facing his troops: the attack against their right to preach and parade in public. He contacted Home Secretary, Sir William Harcourt, providing evidence of magistrates in Worthing refusing to summons those who had assaulted his officers. The attacks in Worthing in 1884 had been so violent and constant, that the General had commanded his officers to cease their open-air meetings for a time. When Harcourt chose not to get involved, asserting that the State had no power over the local authorities, Booth refused to give in. Not to be denied, he gathered more evidence describing how the Skeleton Army in Worthing was supported and funded by prominent community members. Once again Harcourt turned a blind eye.

Furious, but realising he was fighting a lost cause in demanding the assistance of the Home Secretary, Booth finally consented to allow the troops in Worthing under the leadership of Captain Ada, to recommence their Sunday parades. Concerned for his people, he again appealed to Harcourt, informing him of the Army's decision to march.

What followed was one of the most violent and bloody clashes ever made against the Salvation Army. Many of the Skeletons received a court summons for assault and disturbing the peace, but this did not stop them. Over the days that followed, they continued their violent rioting, assaulting police officers, disrupting indoor Army meetings and looting a shop owned by a Salvationist. The mob was further inflamed when its ringleaders were sentenced to a months hard labour for their part in the riots.

A special squadron of 40 guards was eventually called into the village to disperse the rioters and clear the streets. Further clashes occurred over the weeks that followed. However, at long last the police were now clearly in defense of the street marchers. Victory was declared as police notices went up decreeing all Skeleton Army subscribers to be criminals, with the immediate penalty of three months hard labour. The Army had won a decisive victory. To the delight of Captain Ada and her battle-weary troops, the citizens who had previously condoned the attacks against them now rallied together to form a voluntary bodyguard at all open air meetings.

The victory in Worthing signaled the beginning of the end of the intense persecution. As the months went by, other villages adopted a hard-line against the Skeleton Army and reaffirmed the Salvationist's rights to hold public meetings.

The Army emerged from the intense period of persecution battle weary, but stronger than ever before. By 1884, the movement had grown to over 900 corps, with more than 260 of these being overseas. Immigration to places as far flung as America, Canada and Australia had excited the hearts of soldiers seeking a new start in these developing countries. Once settled in their new homelands, they would hold meetings, 'Army style' of course. Immediately people responded to the gospel, word was sent back to Headquarters in London that the

"Hold the standard high, let us tell
the world of the blood and fire."
encouraged the General.

Albert 'Wingy' Hodson, one of the many converted Skeleton Army leaders.

work had been established and reinforcements were required. Officers were hurriedly dispatched with teams of soldiers to support and
oversee the extension of the work in these lands.

The growing number of corps and the widening scope and infiltra-
tion of these young pioneers, saw the Army's annual budget exceed
£30,000 in 1884. Clerical staff at Army headquarters in London frequently received and dispatched up to 2000 letters each day! This
rapid growth stretched resources to the limit and for Booth the problems of support and survival grew more and more intense.

In later years Bramwell Booth remembered the struggle of these
days:

> *"The money burden was never lifted. It remained a heavy cloud
> - perhaps divinely permitted to keep us of a practical turn of mind.
> Of well-to-do friends to whom we could look to for a five pound
> note, he had not about a dozen; and even when they did help
> him they generally wanted to fix their gift for some new effort,
> forgetting (what many people with kind intentions forget today!)
> that the ordinary work has still to be financed, and that the cost
> of the regular organisation cannot be made to disappear by sim-
> ply overlooking it!"* [3]

More than ever before, volunteers had to be prepared for the hardship that accompanied the life of an officer. In 1882, when Booth sent
word out to Salvationists of a team that was soon to leave for India, he
described in detail the difficulties they would face.

"Remember that you are likely to be absolutely alone - it may be for months together... in the villages the men must expect to have no furniture at all, except some mats, and must learn to sit on the ground like a tailor... you will have to learn to cook just as Indians do and to wash your clothes at the stream with them... You must make up your mind to leave entirely forever and behind you all your English ideas and habits..." [4]

The difficulties arising from stretched resources were not confined to officers serving overseas. As early as 1878, Booth had been forced to issue a 'General Order Against Starvation' to ensure the self-sacrificing attitudes of his officers did not lead to ill health or compromise the well-being of their families. In order to meet the expenses required to keep their corps going, officers lived and ate as simply as possible. At times they existed on stale bread crusts and spoiled fruit. Sometimes, for extended periods, they would not eat at all!

Despite these hardships, Booth and his officers persevered with incredible commitment and stamina. No difficulty was allowed to bring the work of salvation to a halt. The state of men's souls was at stake! As the Army stretched out its arms to embrace the world, its members knew more than ever to prepare to pay the price. There was no denying it; the cost was great. Some had already lost their lives in this salvation war. Countless others had given up the right of a comfortable existence, choosing to go without luxuries in order to see others come into the Kingdom of God. Undaunted by poverty or persecution these soldiers of Christ saw 250,000 new converts come to Christ between 1881 and 1885 alone.

Each of them was challenged to follow the example of their leader who had literally given his life for their salvation. William and Catherine laid aside their own rights and dedicated their strength, their gifts, their time, their family and material wealth to the purpose of the Gospel of Jesus Christ. Booth encouraged his followers to lay their own lives down for God, stating:

> *"True courage does not think about self; it rises above self - tramples it beneath its feet. It does not even measure and inquire the value and worth of its object. Enough for it that there is duty to be done, difficulties to be overcome, burdens to be borne and suffering to be relieved; regardless of self, and in a measure regardless of its ability to accomplish the task it sets itself upon, it goes straight at it; 'to do or die' - nay, 'to die and do,' if the doing cannot be done without dying - may it be taken as its motto."* [5]

These are the words of a man who lived in an atmosphere heavily charged with faith and prayer. No limp, languid existence for this persistent fervent spirit. No faint-heartedness, only a courageous tenacity and a wholehearted pushing toward the mark for the high calling of God.

From its conception the atmosphere of the Salvation Army was charged with faith and prayer. Between 1881 and 1885 250,000 new converts came to Christ.

Young pioneers flocked in to see the
saving of souls and the creation of
General William Booth's social
welfare policies.

*Growth is the process of responding positively to
change. Grappling with hardships, trouble, and
calamity; facing adversity in a spirit of determination
and courage; loving and not being crushed by broken
hopes; holding our head high,
having done our best - this is growth.*

UNKNOWN

*We cannot tell what may happen to us in the strange
medley of life. But we can decide what happens in us -
how we take it, what we do with it - and that is what
really counts in the end. How to take the raw stuff of
life and make it a thing of worth and beauty
- that is the test of living.*

JOSEPH FORT NEWTON

CHAPTER FIVE

To Gain, Train

ow wide is the girth of the world?" Booth challenged the huge crowd of Salvationists gathered at a London rally in 1885. "Twenty-five thousand miles," came the rousing response.

Booth feigned thoughtfulness. His hand stroked his flowing beard, the furrows on his brow deepened as his gaze moved steadily across the breadth of the crowd. "Then," he roared thrusting wide his arms, "We must grow till our arms get right round about it."[1]

And grow they did. By this time, the Army was already operating in 11 countries and there was no slowing of its growth. Booth had been unprepared for the rapid expansion, and the burden of responsibility weighed heavily upon him and his family. The cost of training and caring for the multitudes that had pledged their lives to the Army's cause stretched funds beyond their limit. Cheques were often written in faith, with the knowledge that until God provided, the payments couldn't be made. Yet, God was faithful and the money always came in, often from unknown and unexpected sources.

As Booth forged ahead, leading the Army in its quest to evangelise the nations, the importance of training became more and more evident. He was convinced that preparation was an essential key to success.

Training was already a hallmark of his own life. As a young man, he had studied carefully the lives and works of the men and women of God who had achieved any measure of success in the fight against evil. He diligently applied himself, learning all he could from those who forged ahead in the work of God. Recognising early God's evangelistic call on his life, he had hunted the world over to find those who were successful in winning souls. He studied their journeys and the messages they preached, striving to discover the principles and methods that had led to their success.

Booth's strategy and thinking was greatly influenced by revivalists including Wesley, Caughey, Finney, Marsden and others. Intrigued by their faith and persistence, he thoughtfully pondered their achievements and shortcomings. Reminiscing at the age of 80, the still active old general was able to say, "...from the day of my conversion to God I have never read a biography, heard an address, or attended a meeting, without asking myself the question: 'Is there anything here from which I can learn how better to fulfill my own mission in enforcing the claims of my Lord; and saving the souls of men?'" [2]

For Booth, life was for training and training was for life. He endeavoured always to "learn how best to fight the enemies of God and man, bring them to submission, transform them into good soldiers of Jesus Christ, unite them for most effective actions, and lead them forth to combat with the foe."[3]

As a father, he was fully aware of the importance of training his young family. He recognised the remarkable God-given influence of a parent over their offspring and, together with Catherine, he determined to influence each of his uniquely gifted children for God. They were conscious of the importance of instructing their children, by both word and example. As a family, they were always involved together in the work of God's Kingdom, their home constantly bustling with life and activity. Their nine children growing up in an atmosphere of genuine faith. On a daily basis they experienced God through the lives of their parents.

The Booths had a policy of never receiving financial reward from Salvation Army funds and consequently they lived very simply. As a result, the children had a great appreciation and awareness of the struggles faced by many poor families, but they also understood and experienced the wonderful provisions received through prayer. They saw first hand how God supplied finances and resources, including dedicated and valued workers.

Great care was taken to incorporate the children into each aspect of the Army's work. Their participation allowed them to grow personally in knowledge and experience. Together with Catherine, William constantly exhorted his children to follow their example, teaching them from a young age to respond to the call and destiny of God on their lives. As their daughter, Evangeline, once remarked, "My parents did not have to say a word to me about Christianity. I saw it in action."[4]

As each child grew, they, like their father, regarded the salvation of the world as their primary object in life. As they matured, each took on a prominent role in the work of The Salvation Army. Booth's eldest son, Bramwell, began as a teenager to handle the administration and served faithfully as Chief of Staff until his father's death. Ballington and Herbert were involved in fieldwork and the training of cadets. Daughters Kate, Emma and Evangeline were also involved in cadet training and field work in England, France, Switzerland and India. In each of his children, William Booth strove to reproduce his own positive character traits - those of perseverance, sacrifice, hard work and a compassion for the underprivileged.

As a young 23 year old, Booth's eldest daughter, Kate, took up the challenge of reaching France with the gospel. Kate's preaching gift and feisty militant spirit stood her in good stead for the difficulties she faced in this hard and hostile territory. France proved a difficult country to break into. Leading her team of three female Salvationists, she preached night after night to rowdy, drunken audiences with little response. The team received nothing but heckling and criticism for six long wearisome months.

Finally the breakthrough came. This particular evening meeting was disrupted from the first moment by the torments of a woman known locally as 'the devil's wife.' Of immense size, she would stand in the meeting hall her hands on her hips and sleeves rolled up above the elbows; with one wink she would set everybody screaming and yelling. During this particular meeting everything Kate and her lieutenants did or said was ridiculed by 'the devil's wife.' The tone of the meeting grew more and more unruly and soon some of the audience began to dance. The meeting seemed lost, until, by a master-stroke, Kate turned defeat into victory.

Through the riotous din she shouted, "Mes amis! I will give you twenty minutes to dance, if you will give me twenty minutes to speak!" The crowd agreed and after 20 minutes of dancing the busker's music was silenced by the interruption of an outspoken Frenchman who called for Kate to speak.

For an hour and 20 minutes she preached with passion and great authority under the anointing of the Holy Spirit, calling her listeners to genuine repentance and faith in Jesus Christ. A strange silence rested on the people as she spoke. The tide had turned. Hundreds of men and women were saved in the two years that followed. Kate had learned for herself that salvation was indeed 'for all men' and like her parents she committed her life to the work of God with renewed vigour.[5]

Booth was a good father, however he was not perfect. His schedule was constantly busy and he did not always take time for his growing family. He sometimes allowed himself to become so absorbed in his work for God and so distracted by the pressures of ministry that he did not give his children the time and love of a father. In his weakness, he favoured those of his children who worked the hardest and accomplished the most. Results impressed him. His children recalled him being most loving and encouraging towards them during their younger childhood years.

As leader of a dedicated army of volunteers, Booth realised early his potential to 'father' others aside from his own natural children. He was acutely aware of the need to disciple and train his people in a way that would see them grow to reach full maturity.

Even in his early days of holding evangelistic meetings on the Methodist circuit, he was intensely aware of the need to care for new converts. He always ensured the name and address of every one was noted down. He knew the real possibility that these believers could falter in their newfound faith and so he carefully assigned each one to a mature believer for discipleship.

Booth's Methodist background had prepared him well and he built discipleship into the foundations of The Salvation Army. In the early days, weekly visits were made to all new believers for the purpose of teaching and discipleship. It became the duty of every officer to devote three hours each day to visiting converts.

Like their General, many of the soldiers had made a simple start in life. They had little or no education including the practical principles of health and hygiene. The Booths quickly discerned the need to instruct and train the new converts in these and other fundamentals of living. Education in the ways of raising a family, nutrition, hygiene, relationships and being a good employee were deemed to be of great importance. Meetings were held every week for the purpose of teaching new believers on the issues of everyday living.

A monthly publication called *The Salvationist*, which was later distributed weekly as *The War Cry*, became a vital means of disseminating information to Salvationists across the world. The first edition of *The War Cry* was dedicated "...to all those who, obedient to the Master's command, are simply, lovingly and strenuously, seeking to rescue souls..."[6] Booth described its purpose as being, "To inspire and educate, and bind our people together all over the world."[7] The weekly publication became a powerful tool for discipling and informing the troops of developments in The Salvation Army.

As a father, he had learnt the vital lesson that effective training needed to be more than instruction. From the moment of their conversion, believers were therefore encouraged 'to hear' and 'to do.' Booth's aim was to see "Every man saved... and every man at work, always at work to see other people saved."[8] A sense of responsibility for the work of the Gospel rested heavily on every believer.

Although Booth always had a great love for the poor, his time with the Methodist church had not equipped him to effectively communicate to them with the excellence he desired. When he first began the work in East London, it seemed as though a barrier separated him from those he sought so desperately to reach. One evening, while preaching in Whitechapel to a restless, inattentive crowd of about 1200, he called on an old gipsy hawker, who had been converted a few weeks earlier, to testify to what God had done for him. As the old man unfolded his story in a simple yet awkward manner, Booth noted with surprise the hush that fell upon the crowd. He watched in amazement and realised an important truth: a simple street hawker could command the attention of this sort of audience in a way that he could not.

As a result of this observation, he took what was recognised to be a radical step. He began to involve his converts in preaching and discovered that although they lacked education and finesse, the crowds responded enthusiastically to their raw humour and unpolished style. The power and truth of their stories had a great impact on the listeners. Every convert was encouraged to testify to the work of God in their lives and they were immediately involved in the work of spreading the gospel.

Until 1880, no facilities existed for the training of cadets for leadership in The Salvation Army. When William and Catherine moved to a sixteen room home in Clapton Common, their old family home in Hackney was turned into a training school for 30 women cadets under the leadership of daughter Emma. A year later a training home for men was opened, with son Ballington taking charge. In these early facilities the new cadets underwent a seven-week course, which was highly practical and extremely gruelling. The prerequisites for those desiring to undergo officer training were 'great stamina' and 'faith.'

Life in training was lived at a rapid pace and by 1886, when the course was increased to six-months, it was not uncommon for cadets to completely wear out a pair of boots before graduation. Their training was always 'hands-on.' Preaching before abusive crowds, visiting and caring for the sick, preparing their own meagre meals and keeping the 'barracks' in pristine condition were all part of the daily routine for the future officers.

The training focused initially on matters of the heart. When questioned about how they trained their officers, Catherine responded in the following way:

> *"Well we begin with the heart...True, we receive no candidates but such as we have good reason, after careful enquiry, to believe are truly converted. Nevertheless, we find many of them are not sanctified; that is, not having fully renounced the flesh or the world, and not thoroughly given up to God...which we regard as indispensable to the fullness of the Holy Spirit and success in winning souls. In addition to meetings and lectures devoted to heart-searching truths, every cadet is seen privately, talked and prayed with, and counselled according to his or her individual necessi-*

*ties... We take it to be a fundamental principle that if the soul is
not right, the service cannot be right, and therefore we make the
soul first and chief care. Next, instruct the candidates in principles, discipline and methods of The Salvation Army through which
they are to act upon the people. Not only is this done in theory in
the lecture room, but they are led into actual contact with the
ignorance, sins and woes of the people."* [9]

Whilst studying the Bible and devouring Booth's manuals of *Orders
and Regulations* and *Salvation Army Doctrines*, the cadet's most powerful lessons were learned by experience. The second phase of training required future graduates to personally campaign in towns and
villages around England. They were never shielded from the hard re-
alities of leadership in the Army during these campaigns. First hand
experience was gained of the nature and hardships of a field officer's
life.

Through the arduous cadetship, all were prepared for the hard
work that lay ahead of them as officers. "I sentence you all to hard
labour," he joked grimly to one passing-out parade, "for the rest of
your natural lives."[10] The difficulties and persecution were so much a
part of life for Booth and his officers that he knew only those called
and impelled by God would be able to go the distance.

All who came to William and Catherine to enquire about entering
cadet training were left with no doubt as to the totality of the call.

Catherine once spoke to a young woman seeking to become a recruit saying, "Have you thought what it means to cast in your lot with us? As time goes on you will probably see those you love much better than yourself or your own life pushed about or stoned or sent to prison. You will have to see them spoken evil of and written against in the newspapers. You must make up your mind to it all - to it all."[11]

It has been said, "the world knows little about its heroes." Booth, however, was one who recognised the hero potential in his converts. These were the men and women he gave his life to and focused his training upon. Realising his own limitations, he set about reproducing in these officers the character qualities, vision, values and principles necessary for the expansion of the Army's work. In this respect, The Salvation Army was unique and different to many other Christian organisations.

Booth worked tirelessly to produce hardened seasoned veterans of the cross - leaders who were equipped and prepared to train hard, work hard and wage war to bring God's salvation message to the world.

Typical of these was 'God's chimney-sweep,' Elijah Cadman, who as a six-year-old child had answered a "Wanted - Small Boys for Narrow Flues" advertisement and was immediately put to work. The last child in a family of five, unusually small and with no education, Elijah was well suited to such a task.

The General worked tirelessly to
produce hardened, seasoned,
veterans of the cross.

One-time chimney-sweep,
'Fiery Elijah' Cadman.

His life was hard. As a young boy, Elijah was rarely sober and often found in a drunken state crumpled in the corner of a rat-infested alley. By the time he reached the age of 17 he was proud to say, "I can fight like a devil and drink like a fish." But change was about to stare him in the face.

One December day he was watching a public hanging at Warwick. As the execution was carried out Elijah's friend pointed to the dangling bodies and quipped, "That's what you'll come to, 'Lijah, one day!" The sudden realisation of his own guilt was so shocking that he immediately gave up drinking and fighting. He began going from village to village ringing a town crier's bell in front of each inn until a crowd gathered. "This is to give notice, 60,000 people are lost," he would bawl. "Lost! Lost! Lost! Lost every year through the cursed drink. Mr Cadman, the 'Sober Sweep from Rugby', will give an account of his drinking experiences! Come and hear him! Come and hear him!"[12]

Then, when he was 21, Cadman surrendered his life to Christ as he listened to a street-preacher with whom he had intended starting a row. In 1876, he was stunned and challenged as he heard Booth powerfully preach the message of the cross and forthwith joined the growing army of volunteers. Booth recognised the potential preacher and evangelist in Cadman. He looked beyond his past into his future as a child of God. It wasn't long before Cadman and his wife sold their chimney-sweep business, home and other possessions and moved to Hackney in the east of the city to take charge of the work there. Later that year he reported, "We are making a powerful attack on the devil's kingdom... King Jesus is our great Commander...We have an army here that will face the world, the flesh and the devil." A year later Booth sent Cadman to 'open fire' on Whitby, where in no time at all the numbers at Sunday meetings swelled to over 3000.[13]

Such was the fire and passion of these seasoned soldiers. They were warriors of whom it could be said, "They can suffer, they can die, but they cannot flinch; they will not yield."[14]

The General's long sighted vision for the Army extended far beyond his own lifetime. With the future in mind, he sought to instill in his people the principles and values of the Word of God and the Salvation Army. One day he would die, but the Army's purpose must continue in the hearts of those that would follow. Wisely, he lived by the motto, "Don't do the work of a thousand men, get a thousand men to do the work."

To look is one thing.

To see what you look at is another.

To understand what you see is a third.

To learn from what you understand

is still something else.

But to act on what you learn

is all that really matters, isn't it?

EDUCATOR'S DISPATCH.

No statue was ever erected to the memory of a man

or woman who thought it was best to

"let well enough alone."

WATCHMAN - EXAMINER

CHAPTER SIX

A Broken Heart

Christmas Day, 1868, was a turning point for Booth and his family. The day had commenced with an early morning service in Whitechapel. As he made his way home after the meeting, the hopelessness and degradation of the East-End streets bombarded his senses as never before.

The stench of the slums penetrated his nostrils as his eyes took in the magnitude of human suffering and depravity that threatened to overwhelm him. Men and women, already reeling from the effects of alcohol, staggered along the dirty streets. Children clothed in rags, shuffled through the garbage that spilled out from the alleys, hoping to find some discarded morsel of food. Some as young as five, wandered about in a drunken stupor and appeared to be near starvation. He tried desperately to rid himself of the hellish sounds, sights and smells as he reached the sanctuary of his Gore Road home. But his heart was broken.

Although they did not have great wealth, the family Christmas celebrations were memorable, with a special meal, joyful singing and much laughter. This year, however, was different. As he joined in with the children's games, Booth's mind was haunted by the images of the streets. Finally he could bear it no longer and pacing the floor he exclaimed, "I'll never spend another Christmas Day like this again. The poor have nothing but the public house, nothing but the public house!"[1]

The compassion in his heart for the poor in London's East End compelled him to action. The following Christmas the Booths and others distributed 300 dinners to starving families, warming the hearts of many.

The seed of the welfare work of the Salvation Army had been sown in the General's life at a very young age. His own childhood experience of poverty was preparation for this call of God. As a teenager, he and a friend provided for a beggar woman who lived on the streets of Nottingham. They collected money from their friends, found a small cottage and furnished it as a home for this dear lost soul. His heart would often challenge his hands to action. "Love spoken can be easily turned away, but love demonstrated will last for a life-time," he often reminded himself.

The value of every human life was very real; he could not dismiss as worthless any person for whom Christ had died. Acutely aware of the suffering the poor endured, Booth was impelled to care not just for people's spiritual well-being, but also for their physical needs. "You can't expect people whose chief concern is the source of their next meal, or somewhere warm to stay during the icy London winter, to hear and respond to the gospel message. No-one gets a blessing if they have cold feet, and nobody ever got saved while they had tooth-ache!" was his firm challenge to his followers. The physical needs of the masses were great. Sickness and disease were rampant in the poor of Victorian England.

In 1871, Smallpox hit hard at the family when seven year-old Marian caught the feared disease. This left her with permanently impaired sight and considerable disfigurement. Scarlet fever, rheumatic fever, measles, whooping cough, almost every ailment found its way into their home. It was truly a miracle that, in an era when childhood diseases claimed many lives, none of their nine children died in infancy. Ministering as they did to vast numbers of sick and poor, their home was a refuge for many. This was a small part of the cost of their Christian faith. The family believed they were not in the world for themselves, but for others. They would never, at any cost, shut the door.[2]

In 1872, Booth himself became so sick he was unable to work for six months. His doctor urged him to take time to rest, stating that unless his health improved he may never work again! Sixteen year-old Bramwell stepped into the breach and, together with his mother, made sure the Army's forward momentum did not slacken. They forged ahead with the opening of five 'Food For-The-Million' shops where the poor could purchase hot soup any time of the night or day or sit down to a three-course dinner for a very small charge.

Through the understanding gained during his own time of sickness Booth further encouraged his officers to tend to those with physical needs that they visited each week. Practical Christianity was thoroughly instilled into the hearts of those who gave their lives to serve in this 'dead man's' Army.

Despite his love and compassion for people, the General did not set about to build an organisation that provided welfare services. Each work of welfare began as the Salvationists came face to face with situations of overwhelming need.

In 1881, a young prostitute knelt at the Mercy seat toward the conclusion of a meeting surrendering her life to God. She was counselled and ministered to by Mrs Cottrill, one of Booth's officers. Officer Cottrill was faced with an immediate dilemma. What was she to do with this young girl who had just committed her life to Christ? One thing was for sure - if she genuinely wanted to begin her Christian life she could not return 'home.'

Responding to the need, Officer Cottrill took the young girl into shelter by taking her home. As other girls came to Christ, she set aside her basement rooms to house them. In 1883, a refuge home was finally opened in Whitechapel to care for the growing number of girls rescued from prostitution.

In the same year Major James Barker was faced with a similar problem in Melbourne, Australia. His work in the Melbourne Prison had been so successful that a great proportion of his converts were ex-criminals. These men and women begged him to let them help him in the work of his corps.

"Give me a chance," one 60-year old pleaded on his release from prison. "I don't want to die in jail." Barker consented and his chief-of-staff took the old man home, fed him and found him work. One month later, the dying man's final faltering words were, "The Army was like home." When Barker heard this, it suddenly occurred to him that a home was exactly what these ex-criminals needed.

The first Salvation Army Prison Gate Home was opened close to the jail and a vital ministry was born. The Army's work with ex-criminals was so successful the Australian government provided them with funding and the freedom to do whatever they could to help solve the problem of rising unemployment.

Despite the success of their early welfare work with the poor, ex-criminals and young women, Booth was still yet to face his greatest challenges in this area. The first arrived on his doorstep in 1885 in the form of a teenage girl clutching a Salvation Army songbook and demanding to see the General.

Annie Swan was a young village girl from Sussex who had answered a newspaper advertisement and travelled to London to work in private service. On her arrival, she discovered to her horror that she had actually been taken captive, along with other teenage girls and her new 'home' was in fact a brothel. Stumbling on the address of the Salvation Army Headquarters in the back of her treasured songbook one night, she was inspired with the determination to break free. A short time later Annie managed to escape from this 'house of fame' and she found her way to freedom through the Army's care and generosity.

Prostitution permeated every level of Victorian society. The authorities largely turned a blind eye to the practice, preferring to ignore its existence rather than uncover and deal with the problems it caused. In 1882, the legal age of consent was just 13, yet it was feared that many girls as young as ten and 11 were being forced into prostitution. Whilst it was an offence for a woman to solicit a man, the law provided no protection for girls over the age of 13 who might be solicited by a man.

An attempt to raise the legal age of consent to 16 had been thrown out of parliament, with one politician arguing that the age of consent should be lowered to ten! His reasoning - it was difficult for a man having to face a charge without being able to plead the consent of a child! This infuriated the Booths as they recalled the look of innocence in the eyes of their own children and wondered how any human being could justify such a statement.

The girls who had sought refuge in the Army home shared horrific stories of the brutality and appalling treatment they endured in the brothels. Annie Swan's story of deception gave Booth further evidence of the evil nature and the magnitude of the sex trade that brewed below the surface of respectable Victorian society.

At his father's request, Bramwell set about immediately to investigate the situation. He enlisted the support of William T. Stead, editor of the *Pall Mall Gazette*. Together they listened to the testimonies of three young girls who had been rescued from the streets and Rebecca Jarrett, a convert who had previously run a brothel. They heard of traps laid to lure young girls and parents who were so desperate they sold their children into prostitution. As they listened they were appalled by stories of an elaborate system that organised the drugging and trafficking of children around England and into Europe for abuse by the professional, high society, and even the royal, clientele of the brothels. The accounts were unending and heart-rending. At times they would listen in total disbelief at the unfolding of yet another cruel plot to destroy innocent lives... tears flowed.

Bramwell and Stead were sickened by the depravity of a civilised society that allowed and encouraged such horrendous abuse against the innocent. Their hearts broke for the thousands who were trapped in this evil system within their own country and they resolved not sit back and allow this to continue.

Together, they concocted an elaborate and rather dangerous plan to gather enough evidence to present a case that could not be ignored by the authorities. With the help of Rebecca Jarrett, they set about to procure a young girl for Stead, who posed as a well-to-do client of a brothel.

The transaction was completed with ease for the sum of just five pounds - one pound for the girl's mother, two pounds for a friend who assisted in setting up the deal and two pounds for a midwife who performed the customary physical check that was often requested by brothel clientele. The girl's mother fully understood her daughter's fate and was delighted to receive her payment of one pound. It was understood that her father, a convicted thief, was no longer with the family. The whole procedure was carried out as planned, without a hitch.

Armed with all the evidence they required, Stead began to publish a series of articles in the *Pall Mall Gazette*, describing accurately how a young girl had been sold by her family into prostitution. The articles laid out the nature and magnitude of the abuse that was occurring on a daily basis in Britain. The articles were an instant sell-out as the prostitution industry was blown open to public scrutiny.

Within 17 days a petition of 393,000 signatures was carried by Salvation Army cadets to the House of Commons requesting that the age of consent be raised to 18; the procuring of young people for immoral purposes be made a criminal offence; a magistrate be given the power of entry into any house where it is believed that girls are being detained against their will; and it be made a criminal act for a man to solicit a woman. As a result of the petition, the age of consent in England, and in many other countries around the world, was raised to 16.

Through an unwillingness to accept the evils of society, and the courage to challenge the system, this battler and his Army successfully improved the laws of their nation. They set up a national service for helping young girls, including more homes for those rescued from prostitution. Within five years they had 13 homes housing over 300 girls in England and a further 17 homes abroad. Their success, however, did not come without a cost. The mother of the young girl (who was safe and happy in the service of The Salvation Army in France) began to worry about her daughter. She contacted the police and the investigation that followed resulted in charges being laid against Stead and his female accomplice for taking a child from her father without his consent!

As the Army pressed on, reaching out to people who did not know God, the welfare work also continued to grow. To those who saw it all as a carefully planned crusade, Booth responded, "We saw the need. We saw the people starving, we saw people going about half-naked, people doing sweated labour; and we set about bringing a remedy for these things. We were obliged - there was a compulsion. How could you do anything else?"[3]

By 1887, in spite of the successful welfare works already established, Booth remained deeply concerned by the appalling poverty that affronted him as he travelled about his own country. His heart was constantly stirred with compassion by the scores of homeless that huddled amidst scraps of newspaper in the shelter of London Bridge. How could Salvationists merely preach of the love and compassion of God whilst there were men, women and children suffering on his doorstep? Something more had to be done.

Utilising his network of Army officers, who were in touch with the heart and soul of the nation, he began a thorough investigation of the magnitude and nature of the problems that assailed the poor in England. Day after day, reports and statistics poured into Salvation Army Headquarters telling story after story of the plight of the unemployed and the homeless across the nation.

The standard of living was well below what we today term the 'poverty-line' and what Booth referred to as the 'standard of the London cab horse.'

Booth likened the treatment of cab horses working in the streets of London to the basic standard of life that should be experienced by every person. Every cab horse had three things: shelter at night, food to eat, and work to do by which to earn its food. Whenever a cab horse tripped or fell in the middle of traffic in London, people responded immediately to get the animal on its legs again. Immediately the horse was helped up, the harness was taken off and everything done to restore the animal to full strength. There was never any delay as people argued or debated regarding why or how it fell. While the horse lived it had food, shelter and work. This was the very basic standard, which Booth believed must be experienced by every person living in England.

Yet, a horrifying ten percent of the population were experiencing life without this basic standard of food, shelter and work. The government, with little enthusiasm, put in place a few schemes to help. Yet, the only poor these schemes seemed to assist were those who were sober enough, industrious and thoughtful enough to take advantage of the help they offered.

This excluded many of the three million people living in dire poverty. Booth believed that if the State neglected to care for the poor, it was the duty of Christians to take up their cause.

Under the inspiration of the Holy Spirit, and with the help of his officers, a national welfare strategy was developed to address the problem of poverty. With the assistance of William T. Stead, Booth wrote a book entitled *In Darkest England and The Way Out.* In this publication he described the magnitude of poverty in the land. The statistics and stories of those living in 'darkest England,' those who were out of work, without food or shelter and those who resorted to crime in order to live, painted a grim picture. Having described the problems faced by over three million people, he began to outline his strategy to provide assistance for the lost, the homeless and the helpless.

His plan was divided into three parts. Together, he believed they would work to transform the living hell of the homeless into communities of self-helping, self-sustaining families, based on the principles and disciplines of the Salvation Army. The three parts of the *Darkest England* strategy were:

PHASE ONE: THE CITY COLONY

The establishment of institutions to rescue the poor, supply their immediate necessities, provide them with temporary employment and begin to instruct them in godly principles that would assist in life. Some would be re-established in the community through this colony, finding work or being reinstated with family who were able to support and help them. Others would be passed on to the next phase of the strategy.

PHASE TWO: THE FARM COLONY

Those who were unable to find permanent employment in the city would be moved out to a settlement in the country. The reformation of the character of the individuals would continue with education, vocational training and instruction in godly principles and disciplines. Once again, many who were restored in this way would find employment or be reunited with supportive family in other parts of the country. Some would be trained and sent on to the third phase of the strategy.

PHASE THREE: THE COLONY ACROSS THE SEA

At this time in the history of the world, the doors of opportunity were flung wide open for settlement and development of industry in the British colonies of South Africa, Canada and Australia. Booth's strategy included the establishment of a settlement in the colonies which would become the home for some of England's destitute millions.

The *Darkest England* strategy was designed to reach those who could not help themselves. The essential ingredient of any scheme to be developed as part of the strategy was a focus on changing the man, not just his circumstances. Booth was fully convinced the only way to do this was by the power of God. "To get a man soundly saved... it is not enough to put on him a pair of new breeches, to give him regular work, or even to give him a university education. These things are all outside a man, and if the inside remains unchanged you have wasted your labour."[4]

In spite of this belief, the strategy did not force religion on any man. Those who chose not to accept the salvation offered by God received the same practical help as those whose lives were transformed by Jesus Christ.

While Booth laboured over his book, the Army began to implement the schemes that would form part of the strategy. In 1890, they opened Britain's first labour exchange, a full 20 years before the government took up the idea of liaising between the unemployed and those requiring workers. The exchange was a huge success, placing over 69,000 people in employment in just seven years.

Labour yards opened next to each Salvation Army shelter, providing work and a means of restoring self-respect for the unemployed seeking refuge in the shelters. The Army was already proving the worth and success of Booth's welfare strategy.

For this aging saint, the writing of his book was overshadowed by a tragedy of a very personal nature. His wife of almost 40 years was suffering an agonising death from breast cancer. Night after night, William struggled with God as he watched the woman he loved so deeply, suffer great pain and grow weaker by the day. He cried out to God, trying desperately to come to terms with her suffering. Finally he could see the hand of God in the situation and he realised that such trials were valuable as they "recalled God to man and drove men to God."[5]

In spite of her pain, Catherine was a vital part of the formation of the *Darkest England* welfare strategy. Many meetings and discussions were held around her bedside as she encouraged all in their work. When, on a Sunday morning in September 1890, the epic was finally complete, Stead declared prophetically to those gathered around her bed, "That work will echo around the world. I rejoice with an exceeding great joy." Summoning all her strength, Catherine replied in a whisper, "And I most of all. Thank God. Thank God."[6]

Within a few weeks Catherine died in the arms of her beloved husband, surrounded by family and friends. Grief overwhelmed William at the loss of his best friend, and his dearest companion. He knew his success and the success of the Army was largely due to the support

IN DARKEST ENGLAND, AND THE WAY OUT.

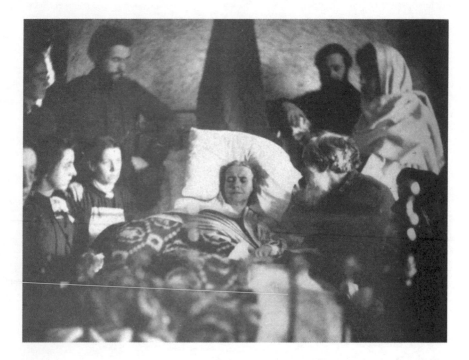

Beloved wife and mother; the family
gather around Catherine's bed-side
during her 'final battle' with cancer.
She went to glory shortly after on
October 4 1890.

and devotion of his wife, and the thought of continuing without her was almost inconceivable. In spite of his loss however, his mission remained unchanged.

Standing at the graveside to address the Salvationists he declared, "My work plainly is to fill up the weeks, the days and the hours and cheer my poor heart as I go along with the thought that when I have served Christ and my generation according to the will of God...then I trust that she will bid me welcome to the skies, as He bade her."[7] When Booth's book, *In Darkest England and the Way Out* was finally released it contained the dedication *"To the memory of the companion, counsellor, and comrade of nearly forty years; the sharer of my every ambition for the welfare of mankind - my loving, faithful and devoted wife."*[8]

Overnight, *In Darkest England and the Way Out* became a bestseller and Booth became the most talked about man in Britain. The timing was perfect; the nation was slowly awakening to the desperate cries of the underprivileged, and reformers including Lord Shaftesbury were joining the fight against poverty. Not everyone however, was supportive of Booth's radical scheme. He suffered intense personal criticism from those who believed social welfare was related only to political and secular theories, not to God or religion. There was great public debate over the issue of the State funding such a scheme.

This lone eagle was once again the focus of slander and accusation. He was labelled "a sensual, dishonest, sanctimonious and hypocritical scoundrel," a "brazen-faced charlatan" and a "masquerading hypocrite."

The words wounded him and Booth clearly felt the full brunt of their attack. Speaking of his many critics he stated, "The day has gone when the priest and Levite are content to pass by the wounded man. They must needs stop now, turn back, and punch the head of any good Samaritan who dares to come to the rescue."[9]

Although their attitude angered him, he had learnt long ago to leave them with God. When Bramwell was angered by the spiteful comments, his father wisely replied, "Bramwell, fifty years hence it will matter very little indeed how these people treated us. It will matter a great deal how we dealt with the work of God."[10] Ignoring his critics, the Army continued to implement his strategy.

Work was provided for the unemployed who entered the scheme. At Hadleigh in Essex, Booth's farm colony was established and thousands of men were equipped with skills that enabled them to find employment in the workforce in England or the colonies. A Missing Persons Bureau was developed to help families trace their loved ones. Plans were made for a legal aid service for the poor and a Poor Man's Bank with credit facilities for the establishment of new businesses by the unemployed.

There was hardly a need in the community that was not in some way catered for under the *Darkest England* scheme. Although successful in many ways, the scheme was fraught with difficulties. The public had pledged an initial £100,000 to implement the programme, however the required annual contribution of £30,000 did not eventuate.

Rumours were spread suggesting Booth was helping himself to the funds that had been provided. After a thorough investigation by an independent committee of five auditors, it was concluded that he had never drawn an income from mission or Army funds. Despite being cleared of this charge, the damage was done and the scheme suffered from a continual funding shortfall. The overseas colony was never established, due in part to a lack of finance.

Despite the setbacks, some aspects of this pioneering work were gradually accepted by England and other nations including Australia, France, Germany, Holland, India and America. The scheme fashioned by the Salvation Army became in part a blueprint for the welfare services implemented and supported by the governments of these nations.

Although Booth did not set out to create a social welfare machine, his love for God and the compassion in his heart for his fellow man compelled him to provide for the physical needs of those he sought to reach. The purpose of his life - the salvation of men and the extension of the Kingdom of God - remained unchanged.

As he lived in obedience to God, his life's purpose was outworked by the practical works of his faith. Booth was a man whose faith was clearly evident as he fed the hungry, housed the homeless and provided a 'hand up' for the poor. His compassion for the lost, the destitute and the helpless never left him and he laboured to bring them assistance and answers through the practical gospel of Jesus Christ.

*Prayer must be clothed with fervency, strength, and power. It is
the force that, centred on God, determines the amount of
Himself given out for earthly good. Men who are fervent in
spirit are bent on obtaining righteousness, truth, grace, and all
other sublime, powerful graces that adorn the character of the
authentic, unquestioned child of God.*

E. M. BOUNDS

*Go back, back to the upper room; back to your knees; back to
searching of the heart and habit, thought and life, back to
pleading, praying, waiting, till the spirit of The Lord floods the
soul with light, and you are endued with power from on high.
Then go forth in the power of Pentecost, and the Christ life
shall be lived, and the works of Christ shall be done. You shall
open blind eyes, cleanse foul hearts, break men's fetters, and
save men's souls. In the power of the Spirit, miracles become
the commonplace of daily living.*

SAMUEL CHADWICK

*A travailing spirit, the throes of a great burdened desire,
belong to prayer. A fervency strong enough to drive away sleep,
which devotes and enflames the spirit, and which retires all
earthly ties, all this belongs to wrestling, prevailing prayer. The
Spirit, the power, the air and food of prayer is in such a spirit.*

ADONIRAM JUDSON

CHAPTER SEVEN

Prayer, Faith and the Power of the Spirit

en take up religion with the tips of their fingers, as a matter of little or no importance; worthy of being considered and attended to, but only in its place - and that mainly on the Sabbath, and always in subordination to considerations of reputation and pleasure and gain. No wonder that such persons make no progress and have no strength, and find no inward peace and gladness in the Saviour's cause." [1]

Booth's description of the state of many churchgoers in Victorian England, although not complimentary, was quite accurate. His growing Army of salvation soldiers were of a different breed. Grasping hold of God with both hands, they fought hard for the expansion of God's Kingdom in every part of the world. Undergirding all their efforts was the power of prayer.

In every aspect of life, Booth was an advocate and an example of wholehearted prayer and living. With all his heart, he believed the Bible - the Word of God. With all his might he took hold of the God of the Word. As he did, his life became a testimony to the miraculous. This rugged-cross-carrier knew what it was to fight the fight of faith.

Obstacles and difficulties were frequently before him. Sickness, grief, financial pressure, physical persecution, slander and public criticism were commonplace, and in the midst of such problems, he strove after a full trust in God. Seizing the opportunities each problem presented, time after time, he would throw himself upon God, boldly relying on His protection, provision and direction. As faith rose within, he experienced over and over again the miraculous provision and power of a faithful God. His determined faith overflowed as a life of prayer.

From the early years, prayer was foundational to Booth and his ministry. Prayer undergirded every aspect of his life and his relationships - with God, with Catherine, with his family, his followers and the people he strove to reach. It was commonplace in the Booth household. When Catherine accepted his proposal of marriage, they knelt together in her parent's home, giving themselves to each other and to God. Years later, their children would recall how often they saw their parents hand-in-hand, kneeling in prayer for strength, courage, provision or protection - whatever their need they would seek God until the answer came.

Prayer was a vital aspect of the Army's corporate meetings. Organised prayer was held for children and adults, in the mornings and at mid-day. Half-night and all-night prayer gatherings were frequent. Prayers of intercession were made at the penitent-form during altar calls to pray people into the Kingdom. Salvationists would often kneel in alleys or streets to pray and intercede for the local community. Booth encouraged his people to pray anywhere, at any time, in everyday language. Writing on the value of his prayer life in his New Years Eve address in 1906, he stated:

"O' when I look back over the course I have travelled through the world, my comrades, what a precious invaluable privilege prayer has been to me! Were I, while I write this, again standing on the threshold of my earthly life, whether long or short, I should at once start to pray. I should pray alone in my chamber, with my family, in my home, with friends when I met them, with strangers, in halls, open-air meetings, or elsewhere. Indeed, I should pray in public and in private; yes, everywhere I should pray, until my every thought was prayer and my every breath was praise." [2]

Convinced of its unequalled value and importance, he urged his followers to give themselves unreservedly to prayer.

"You must pray with your might. That does not mean saying your prayers, or sitting gazing about in church or chapel, with eyes wide open, while someone else says them for you. It means

fervent, effectual, untiring wrestling with God. It means that grappling with Omnipotence, that clinging to Him, following Him about, so to speak, day and night, as the widow did to the unjust judge, with agonising pleadings and arguments and entreaties, until the answer comes and the end is gained. This kind of prayer be sure the devil and the world and your own indolent, unbelieving nature will oppose. They will pour water on this flame. They will ply you with suggestions and difficulties. They will ask you how you can expect that the plans and purposes and feelings of God can be altered by your prayers. They will talk about impossibilities and predict failures; but, if you mean to succeed, you must shut your ears and eyes to all but what God has said, and hold Him to His own word: and you cannot do this in any sleepy mood; you cannot be a prevailing Israel unless you wrestle as Jacob wrestled, regardless of time aught else, save obtaining the blessing sought - that is, you must pray with your might." [3]

Through prayer Booth wrestled with God time and again and encouraged his followers to do the same. During their prayer meetings they experienced the heart-wrenching cries and groans of intercession as they sought His face. Booth never waned in his passion for the salvation of the harassed and downtrodden masses. He wept for them on his knees and gained through prayer the compassion and power that infused his preaching. He encouraged Salvationists to involve themselves in their own soul-shaking prayer.

The story is told of two struggling officers who tried everything they could think of to establish a new work, but all to no avail. The opposition was fierce and relentless; they were ready to quit. Weary and discouraged they wrote to Booth, requesting the closure of their station. Booth responded by telegram with just two words... 'try tears'... they did, and revival broke out![4] Like many other Salvationists, they experienced for themselves the power of the fervent prayer of the righteous.

In October 1891, Booth's handpicked team of five young officers was sent to wage war in Zululand, South Africa. Led by Scottish born Captain Allister Smith, the team settled amongst the Zulu warriors on the shore of the Amatikulu River in October 1891. The nature of their opposition was evident from the outset. The Zulu chief and his people revered the powerful witch doctors whose occult practises struck great fear in their hearts. Smith and his team realised that while the witch doctors reigned over the lives of the Zulu, progress of the gospel would be minimal.

They went to 'knee drill,' crying out to God for the release of the Zulu to the gospel of Christ. The atmosphere was so heavily charged with resistant forces that their prayer by necessity contained 'heat, fire and abundant passion.' These young dedicated warriors were no strangers to this form of impassioned prayer.

Their breakthrough opportunity came in August 1892 as drought ravaged the Amatikulu district. When the Zulu's most powerful 'rain doctor' failed to bring an end to the drought, the Chief sent word to Captain Smith saying, "Our hearts are dried up within us. Our courage is finished. The Great One has called the rain doctor, but he has failed to overcome the dry devil who beats us with his rod of hot air."

The request of the chief was presented to Smith: if the Army would hold a Sunday prayer meeting to Great-Great, the White Man's God, all the Chief's people would be ordered to attend.

Boldly, Smith sent word back to the Chief, informing him of their willingness to pray for rain in a public meeting on Sunday. What a challenge. Here was an opportunity for the power of God to be displayed. Answered prayer would almost certainly bring the breakthrough they were praying for, but what would happen if their prayers went unanswered?

Richard Collier, in his book *The General Next to God*, relates the story of this 'Mount Carmel' experience.

> *"No officer in Booth's Army ever prayed harder than Smith did now. Sunday saw hundreds of Zulus trudging across the parched valleys and plains, squatting on the forlorn brown grass outside the Catherine Booth settlement. To his secret joy, Smith saw that at least one Zulu, despite the crowd's scoffing, had brought a vast umbrella.*

> *"You could shelter your family under that tent, Jojo! Do you think it will rain?" As the banter died, the upright old man re-*

plied demurely: "Well, we are here today to pray for rain, and it might rain!" It was an answer, Smith thought, to shame many a Christian.

Then, rising before his vast audience, he taught them a short simple prayer in the Zulu tongue: "Our Lord, send upon us the rain in Thy mercy. Help us with rain. Shower it upon us, O Great-Great."

At once, Smith's handful of converts began fervently to pray. Uncertain at first, the Zulus followed. Voices rose and fell in exhortation, dying sometimes to a mumble as one man prayed alone, rising again in massed volume to seek God's intervention. Three hours passed. The sun was white and pitiless in a blue, brassy sky and Smith prayed on.

Suddenly, from far to the east, towards the Indian Ocean, came a heavy rumbling. Rapt with awe the congregation saw, piling inland from the sea, massed thunderheads moving inexorably towards Amatikulu. The sun from the west blazed upon them and they shone like high and snow-capped ridges.

As the thunder rolled louder, louder rose the prayers. Feet away from Smith, a searing flash of forked lightning ripped the ground. Again thunder crashed, unbearably loud, drowning out all human sound. In solemn silence the congregation crouched.

Nkulu-nkulu, the Great-Great, was speaking with a warrior's majesty. Warm, wet drops of rain, as large as pennies, spattered on the Zulus' upturned faces. Hastily, with a last devout prayer, Smith brought the meeting to a close: soon the rivers and streams on the homeward journey would be raging white torrents.

He dared not of course, look ahead to a moment, not far distant, when Chief Tshingwayo and all his kraal, even the witch doctors, would themselves profess salvation. Nor could he envisage the first Army-sponsored Zulu school, where pupils from six to sixty came to learn not only to read and write but brick making and husbandry. Fat oxen, broken into the yoke, drew ploughs, which The Army helped the Zulus to purchase. The unfair burdens thrust on the women became properly those of men... All this lay in the future.

On this August Sunday, Smith saw only the people rise and run in all directions, laughing and singing as the rain their prayers had brought beat on their naked bodies. Louder than any sang old Jojo, trudging homeward beneath the vast canopy of an umbrella justified by faith." [5]

Captain Smith and his team, like their beloved leader, knew and experienced the power of prevailing prayer. Encouraged by the General, Salvationists in service all over the world, learnt to surrender themselves completely to God in prayer.

The Army's assault on New Zealand was no different. In response to a letter containing a donation of £200, from Miss Arabella Valpy, from the South Island city of Dunedin, and the request of an Auckland printer, Mr John Brome, the General assigned a team to establish the work of the Army in New Zealand.

On January 11 1883, 20-year old Captain George Pollard and 19-year old Lieutenant Edward Wright, set sail for New Zealand. Like many other officers sent out to attack the world, they were young, but Booth was not concerned about the youthfulness of his pioneers. "It is only war that can make veterans," he told the officers at their farewell. When they reached Melbourne, Australia, they commissioned three other officers to join them in the battle for New Zealand.

The officers arrived at Bluff, the southernmost port in New Zealand on the *SS Manapouri*, on Easter Monday 1883. Pollard later wrote, "We arrived with no friends and very little money, but with abundant confidence in God for the victory."

The Salvation Army 'opened attack' on Invercargill, a town of 8000 in the deep-south on September 9, 1883. Their base of operations was the Theatre Royal, appropriately renamed 'Salvation Theatre.'

The first volley of the attack was 'knee drill' - prayer meetings. In his book, *Sallies of the South*, Neil Reinsborg records the rapid rise of prayer in this city:

> *Week one: Sunday September 9, day of "opening attack." At the 7am "knee drill" 100-110 people turned out. The 11am, 3pm and 7pm services finished with ten salvations. On Monday night one soul was saved; Tuesday, 20 people saved; Wednesday, 12; Thursday, 17; Friday, 19; Saturday, 12. Total Salvations for the first week, 91 people.*

General William Booth, addressing a
large crowd on his visit to inspect
the work in New Zealand.

New Zealand's Salvation Army
youthful pioneers, Captain and Mrs
George Pollard (left), with Captain
and Mrs Ted Wright.

Week two: Sunday September 16, 186 people attended "knee drill." The results that week: 173 souls saved.

The prayer attack continued. By the following Sunday, numbers had swelled to 300. One week later the infantry of intercessors had grown to 700. The General's influence and his consistent orders to "pray, pray, pray," had penetrated the minds of his troops and forged a path to their knees.

The great success of the Army of believers that followed Booth is testimony to the power of God released through persevering prayer. It is testimony also to the presence and power of the Holy Spirit in their lives.

Throughout his life, William Booth desired to be a vessel, filled and overflowing with the Spirit of God. Writing of this desire as one of the resolves by which he would choose again to live his life, he stated,

> *"I should be a man possessed of the Holy Ghost. When men heard my name they would think about God. When they saw me, they would ask themselves: 'Am I doing my duty by my soul?' When they knew I was coming their way, they would feel here is another chance of salvation. I should seek to be filled with the Spirit and aspire, like the apostles of old, to go about the world imparting the Holy Spirit, and breathing forth light and hope and power on the souls of men... I should be an exemplification of the Master's prophecy that out of him should flow rivers of living water."* [6]

Like Finney, Caughey and other revivalists, Booth's preaching and ministry were marked from the outset by the power and presence of the Spirit of God. Manifestations of the Holy Spirit were frequent in the revival services he conducted, unexpectedly, congregational members would fall from their seats and lay shaking on the floor. Others audibly crying out for God's mercy. Frequently meetings would erupt with uncontrollable weeping as God's Word was preached. Together with Catherine, he sought to encourage the work of the Spirit in the lives of believers, whilst guarding against what they termed "mere animal excitement" and unreal or superficial experiences. They did not want to "miss the impossible by looking for the incredible," their feet were kept firmly on the ground.

Booth was thoroughly convinced that no amount of human training, skill or eloquence could take the place of the Holy Spirit's power operating through their lives. He knew the work of God by the Holy Spirit was the only thing that would make a true and lasting difference in the hearts and minds of those he was reaching. As Catherine once stated, "Whatever else there is or is not, there must be the equipment of the Holy Ghost, for without Him, all qualifications... are utterly powerless for the regeneration of mankind."[7]

The centrality of the Holy Spirit in Booth's life and work was represented on the first Army banner as the central gold star on which was the words "Blood and Fire." As Catherine presented these banners to new corps in 1879 she proclaimed,

"This flag is a symbol of our devotion to our great Captain...and to the great purpose for which He... shed His blood, that He might redeem men and women from sin and death and hell... This flag is... an emblem of victory... By what power is this victory going to be achieved? By fire! The Holy Ghost... this fire of the Spirit can transform us as it did Peter... Let all go that occupies the room which the Holy Ghost might fill in your souls... charge on the hosts of hell, and see whether they will not turn and flee!" [8]

Great faith, and unswerving perseverance were consistent marks of Booth's personal and public life. They were undoubtedly the secret of his success.

A leader is great, not because of his or her power,
but because of his or her ability to empower others.
Success without a successor is failure.

JOHN MAXWELL

CHAPTER EIGHT

Finishing the Race

On October 26 1905, 700 officers and four Army bands accompanied Booth as he marched through the streets of London to Guild Hall. Here, the 76-year old patriarch was awarded the honour of 'The Freedom of the City of London' by the Lord Mayor. It seemed Booth's years of struggle against slander, negativity and scepticism were finally over. He was honoured in cities all across England. The University of Oxford esteemed him for his "noble work... a work excelled in range and beneficence by no living man."[1] Social and political leaders, who only ten years earlier had branded him a heretic, a fool and a fraud, now honoured him as they saw with their own eyes the hard won success achieved by the Army. The press, who for years had followed his movement, publishing scathing reports and criticisms, now praised his work. Booth humoured them as always when they came to hear him preach, fixing his gaze on them as he prayed a blessing on those "who always arrive late, leave early and never give anything to the collection."[2]

For most people this would be a time to relax, a time to enjoy the fruit of a lifetime of self-sacrificing service to God. Not so for this old English bulldog. No amount or degree of honour from man deterred him from what remained his primary call - the work of salvation. His heart still grieved passionately for those who did not know Jesus. He was determined that as long as he had breath he would continue to preach the gospel.

In August 1904, inspired by the introduction of the motorcar, Booth set out on the first of a series of six motor campaigns. In just 29 days his six-car procession rattled and bounced its way over 1,224 miles as he preached in 164 meetings across England. The going was tough for his younger companions, let alone for this 75 year old saint. The thick dust of the unsealed, rut-ridden roads filled every pore of their skin. The ride was extremely rough and at times perilously dangerous. "Choose your route carefully" he joked with his driver, "we may be in it for the next twenty miles."

The impact of this novel touring method was totally astounding. All over the country, packed crowds lined the highways to greet the old man in the peaked motoring cap who was fast becoming a national icon. The impact of Booth's preaching was even greater.

It was as though he knew his time was coming to a close and the unfinished task of preaching the gospel to all creation seemed to grip him. With great zeal for God and an ever-increasing passion for souls,

In August 1904, inspired by the
introduction of the motorcar, Booth
set out on the first of six motor
campaigns throughout England.

Enthusiastic crowds across England,
lined the streets to catch a glimpse
of the old general in the peaked cap.

Booth implored men, women and children to surrender themselves to the living Christ. Thousands responded to his desperate pleas.

Although battle scarred and weary his campaigning in the twilight years was not restricted to his own nation. He travelled extensively overseas until his 83rd birthday, preaching in Canada, Japan, the United States, Europe and Russia.

His eyesight was fading as his final years drew to a close. So dimmed was his vision that whilst preaching the pulpit rail would often find itself firmly in the grasp of those hands that had offered hope, comfort and love to thousands. With just the slightest hesitation he would steady and guide himself along the pulpit rail as he poured forth his pleadings for the desperate need of his fellow man. A failed cataract operation had already resulted in the removal of his right eye. His voice was also weakening after years of passionate preaching without the support of public address systems. His strength was now failing fast.

General William Booth's final address was given on the occasion of the public celebration of his 83rd birthday at Royal Albert Hall, London on May 9, 1912. Standing before the crowd of 7000 salvationists, he delivered what was perhaps his most famous speech.

"I might have chosen as my life's work the housing of the poor. That, in early life, presented itself to me as a most important question... I honour those who are devoting themselves to the solution

of the problem. But has not The Salvation Army done something in this direction? If you look abroad, you will find hundreds and thousands up and down the world who tonight have comfortable homes through the influence of the Army...

I might have given myself up to the material benefit of the working classes. I might have drawn attention to the small rate of wages and striven to help them in that direction. But have we not done something for them? Are there not tens of thousands who, but for the Army, might have been almost starved? If we have not done much in the way of increasing income, have we not done a great deal in inculcating principles of economy and self-denial, which have taught the poor a better use of their wages? Their total abstinence from drink, tobacco, gambling and wasteful finery has made hundreds of thousands of people better off than they were before they came under our influence.

I might also have given myself up to promoting temperance reform. This is a most important business. Drunkenness seems to be the curse of every civilised nation under the sun; and I have all my life honoured the men and women who have devoted them-selves to the solving of that problem. But has not The Salvation Army done something in that direction? Every Salvationist all the world over is a strict abstainer from intoxicating liquor, and the children are growing up to follow in their parent's footsteps...

I might have chosen as my life's object the physical improvement and health of the people by launching out on a medical career. As a matter of fact, I think the medical system is capable of improvement, and if I had been a doctor I should certainly have paid more attention to diet than to drugs... We have done something in the way of medical aid, and possess at the present time twenty-four hospitals, while others are coming into existence, and there is no knowing to what extent the enterprise will reach in this direction. As it is, we deal with thousands of patients every year.

I might have chosen to devote my life to the interests of the criminal world. The hundreds of thousands of poor wretches who are pining in the prison cells while we are sitting here at ease, ought to have our sympathy and help... Some 178 women prisoners have been admitted to our homes in this country during the year, and of these 130 have proved satisfactory. We have done something for the criminal, but it is only the commencement of a mighty work the Army is destined to do for the unhappy class.

I might have carried out my consecration for the improvement of the community by devoting myself to politics... I saw something better than belonging to either party and, that by being the friend of every party, I was far more likely to secure the blessing of the multitude and the end I had in view.

And the object I chose all those years ago embraced every ef-fort, contained in its heart the remedy for every form of misery and sin and wrong to be found upon the earth, and every method of reclamation needed by human nature..." [3]

In bringing the meeting to a close, Booth concluded with what were to become his final words to his beloved soldiers:

"And now, comrades and friends, I must say goodbye. I am going into dry-dock for repairs, but the Army will not be allowed to suffer, either financially or spiritually, or in any other way by my absence; and in the long future I think it will be seen - I shall not be here to see, but you will - that the Army will answer every doubt and banish every fear and strangle every slander, and by its marvellous success show to the world that it is the work of God and that the General has been His servant...

While women weep, as they do now, I'll fight; while little chil-dren go hungry, as they do now, I'll fight; while men go to prison, in and out, in and out, as they do now, I'll fight; while there is a drunkard left, while there is a poor lost girl upon the streets, while there remains one dark soul without the light of God, I'll fight - I'll fight to the very end!" [3]

Booth had laboured tirelessly for the salvation of mankind for the 22 years since the death of his beloved Catherine. Finally, his physical body could hold out no longer. A cataract operation on his left eye rendered the old General completely without sight. Having done all he could for God with his sight, he was keen to see what he could do for God as a blind man. He knew, that death was near. His children and friends visited him and he implored them all, especially Bramwell, to press ahead, fulfilling the destiny that had been entrusted to the Salvation Army. On Sunday August 18, he slipped into unconsciousness and death drew near. Quietly, on Tuesday, August 20, 1912, Booth's shallow breathing ceased. A "Blood and Fire" banner draped across his bed lay motionless.

A simple placard placed in the window of the International Headquarters of The Salvation Army announced the news to the world: "The General Has Laid Down His Sword. God is with us."

Over the next three days, the nation of England paid homage to the life of a man who had changed the course of history. 150,000 people filed past the casket that held the General's earthly remains. His funeral service on Tuesday, August 27, was attended by close to 40,000 people. Army officers from around the world stood shoulder-to-shoulder with the destitute and homeless as they rededicated their lives to God's service.

Queen Mary, who decided to attend the funeral at the last minute, was seated amongst the people - there was no time to arrange special seating for her and Lord Shaftesbury. Beside her, on the aisle seat, was a poor, but neatly dressed woman who discreetly placed three faded red carnations on the casket as it passed by. The woman was a prostitute who had been rescued from the slavery of a life of sin by the Salvation Army. Quietly she shared her story with the Queen and murmured gratefully, "He cared for the likes of us." [4]

The following day, the funeral procession of 10,000 Salvationists and 40 Army bands slowly wound through the streets of London from International Headquarters to Abney Park Cemetery. The flags of the world saluted him at half-mast as the entire nation came to a standstill.

Bramwell Booth stood by the graveside. The day after Booth's death, he had been announced as the second General of The Salvation Army. According to Army constitution formed many years before, the departing General was responsible for the appointment of his successor. William Booth's nomination of his son as the second General of the Salvation Army was dated August 12, 1890.

Now, as the casket carrying the earthly body of this stately warrior was lowered into the ground, the man groomed to lead the Army onward in its campaign for the salvation of all mankind, tightened his grasp on the leadership baton. General William Booth's race was over; his successor's had just begun.

23rd May 1912. Last known
photograph of General Booth, as he
anxiously awaited news of pending
surgery, that would cost him his
sight. His dog, 'faithful, Pat' sits at
his feet.

Amongst the crush of the huge crowd, Queen Mary and Lord Shaftesbury found themselves sitting next to a prostitute. Rescued from a life of sin she was one of the hundreds of thousands whose overwhelming gratitude flowed forth unrestrained. As she shared her story with the Queen, she lent over and whispered "he cared for the likes of us."

Prior to Tuesday, 27th August, the
day of the funeral service, 150,000
filed past the casket that held the
General's earthly remains. London
came to a stand-still as England
mourned the passing of one of its
most courageous sons.

A vision that thrusts a man's encapsulated heart out
into the unfathomable realms of human depravity
and causes an immediate active response
is truly a vision of profound significance.
Only the Father's heart knows the depth of love
that emanates from such a life.

TREVOR   YAXLEY

CHAPTER NINE

Who Cares?

The following vision was given to William Booth in 1885. It is reproduced here as written in *The War Cry*, June 20, 1885.

THE VISION - "WHO CARES"

I saw a dark and stormy ocean. Over it the black clouds hung heavily; through them every now and then vivid lightning flashed and loud thunders rolled, while the winds moaned, and the waves rose and foamed and fretted and broke and rose to foam and fret and break again.

In that ocean I thought I saw myriads of poor human beings plunging and floating, shouting and shrieking, cursing and struggling and drowning; and as they cursed and shrieked, they rose and shrieked again, and then sank to rise no more.

And out of this dark angry ocean I saw a mighty rock that rose up with its summit towering high above the black clouds that overhung the stormy sea; and all round the base of this rock I saw a vast platform; and on to this platform I saw with delight a number of the poor, struggling, drowning wretches continually climbing out of the angry ocean; and I saw that a number of those who were already safe on the platform were helping the poor creatures still in the angry waters to reach the same place of safety.

On looking more closely I found a number of those who had been rescued scheming and contriving by ladders and ropes and boats and other expedients more effectually to deliver the poor strugglers out of this sea. Here and there were some who actually jumped into the water, regardless of all consequences, in their eagerness to "rescue the perishing"; and I hardly know which gladdened me most - the sight of the poor people climbing on to the rocks, and so reaching the place of safety, or the devotion and self-sacrifice of those whose whole being was wrapped up in efforts for their deliverance.

And as I looked I saw that the occupants of that platform were quite a mixed company. That is, they were divided into different "sets" or castes and occupied themselves with different pleasures and employments; but only a very few of them seemed to make it their business to get the people out of the sea.

But what puzzled me most was the fact that though all had been rescued at one time or another from the ocean, nearly everyone seemed to have forgotten all about it. Anyway, the memory of its darkness and danger no longer troubled them. Then what was equally strange and perplexing to me was that these people did not seem to have any care - that is, any agonizing care - about the poor perishing ones who were struggling and drowning before their eyes, many of whom were their own husbands and wives, mothers and sisters and children.

And this unconcern could not have been the result of ignorance, because they lived right in sight of it all and talked about it sometimes, and regularly went to hear lectures in which the awful state of the poor drowning creatures was described.

I have already said that the occupants of this platform were engaged in different pursuits. Some of them were absorbed night and day in trading, in order to make gain, storing up their savings in boxes, strong rooms and the like.

Many spent their time in amusing themselves with growing flowers on the side of the rock; others in painting pieces of cloth, or in playing music, or in dressing themselves up in different styles and walking about to be admired.

Some occupied themselves chiefly in eating and drinking, others were greatly taken up with arguing about the poor drowning creatures in the sea and as to what would become of them in the future, while many contented themselves that they did their duty to the perishing creatures by the performance of curious religious ceremonies.

On looking more closely I found that some of the crowd who had reached the place of safety had discovered a passage up the rock leading to a higher platform still, which was fairly above the black clouds that overhung the ocean, and from which they had a good view of the mainland not very far away, and to which they expected to be taken off at some distant day. Here they passed their time in pleasant thoughts, congratulating themselves and one another on their good fortune in being rescued from the stormy deep, and singing songs about the happiness that would be theirs when they should be taken to the mainland, which they imagined they could plainly distinguish just "over there."

And all this time the struggling, shrieking multitudes were floating about in the dark sea quite near by - so near that they could easily have been rescued. Instead of which there they were, perishing in full view, not only one by one, but sinking down in shoals, every day, in the angry water.

And as I looked, I found that the handful of people on the platform whom I had observed before were still struggling with their rescue work. O God, how I wished there had been a multitude of them! Indeed, the toilers seemed to do little else but fret and weep, and toil and scheme for the perishing people. They gave themselves no rest, and sadly bothered everyone they could get at around them by persistently entreating them to come to their assistance. In fact, they came to be voted a real nuisance by many quite benevolent and kind-hearted people, and by some who were very religious too. But still they went on, spending all they had and all they could get on boats and rafts, drags and ropes, and every other imaginable device they could invent for saving the poor, wretched, drowning people.

A few others did much the same thing at times, working hard in their way; but the people who chiefly attracted my attention were at the business all the year round; indeed, they made such a terrible to-do about it and went at it with such fierceness and fury, that many even of those who were doing the same kind of work, only in a milder way, were quite angry with them and called them mad.

And then I saw something more wonderful still. The miseries and agonies, perils and blasphemies of these poor struggling people in the dark sea moved the pity of the great God in Heaven; moved it so much that He sent a Great Being to deliver them. And I thought that this Great Being whom Jehovah sent came straight from His palace, right through the black clouds, and leaped right into the raging sea among the drowning, sinking people; and there I saw Him toiling to rescue them, with tears and cries, until the sweat of His great anguish ran down in blood. And as He toiled and embraced the poor wretches, and tried to lift them on to the rock, He was continually crying to those already rescued - to those who He had helped up with His own bleeding hands to come and help Him in the painful and laborious task of saving their fellows.

And what seemed to me most passing strange was that those on the platform to whom He called, who heard His voice and felt they ought to obey it - at least, they said they did - those who loved Him much and were in full sympathy with Him in the task He had undertaken - who worshipped Him, or who professed to do so - were so taken up with their trades and professions, and money-saving and pleasures, and families and circles, and religions and arguments about it, and preparations for going to the mainland, that they did not attend to the cry that came to them from this wonderful Being who had Himself gone down into the sea. Anyway, if they heard it they did not heed it; they did not care; and so the multitude went on struggling and shrieking and drowning in the darkness.

And then I saw something that seemed to me stranger than anything that had gone before in this strange vision. I saw that some of these people on the platform, who this wonderful Being wanted to come and help Him in His difficult task, were always praying and crying to Him to come to them.

Some wanted Him to come and stay with them, and spend His time and strength in making them happier.

Others wanted Him to come and take away various doubts and misgivings they had respecting the truth of some letters, which He had written them.

Some wanted Him to come and make them feel more secure on the rock - so secure that they would be quite sure they should never slip off again. Numbers of others wanted Him to make them feel quite certain that they would really get on to the mainland some day; because, as a matter of fact, it was well known that some had walked so carelessly as to miss their footing, and had fallen back again into the stormy waters.

So these people used to meet and get as high up the rock as they could; and, looking toward the mainland, where they thought the Great Being was, they would cry out, "Come to us! Come, and help us!" And all this time He was down amongst the poor struggling, drowning creatures in the angry deep, with His arms around them, trying to drag them out, and looking up - oh! so longingly, but all in vain - to those on the rock, crying to them, with His voice all hoarse with calling, "Come to me! Come, and help Me!"

BOOTH'S EXPLANATION OF THE VISION

And then I understood it all. It was plain enough. That sea was the ocean of life - the sea of real, actual, human existence.

That lightning was the gleaming of piercing truth coming from Jehovah's Throne. That thunder was the distant echoing of the wrath of God. Those multitudes of people shrieking, struggling, agonizing in the stormy sea, were the thousands and thousands of ... ungodly people of every kindred, tongue and nation.

Oh, what a black sea it was! And, oh, what multitudes of rich and poor, ignorant and educated were there, and all so unlike in their outward circumstances and conditions, yet all alike in one thing - all sinners before God; all held by, and holding on to some iniquity, fascinated by some idol, the slaves of some devilish lust, and ruled by some foul fiend from the bottomless pit!

"All alike in one thing?" Nay, in two things - not only the same in their wickedness but, unless rescued, alike in their sinking, sinking, sinking; down, down, down to the same terrible doom.

That great sheltering rock represented Calvary; and the people on it were those who had been rescued; and the way they employed their energies and gifts and time represented the occupations and amusements of those who profess to be rescued from sin and Hell and to be followers of Jesus Christ. The handful of fierce, determined saviours were salvation soldiers, together with a few others who shared the same spirit. That mighty Being was the Son of God, "the same yesterday, and today, and for ever," who is still struggling to save the dying multitudes about us from this terrible doom of damnation, and whose voice can be heard... calling on the rescued to come and help Him to save the world.[1]

An artist's early depiction of General
William Booth's strategy that
evolved from his vision.

Born in Britain in 1946, Trevor grew up in the South End of London
before migrating to New Zealand at the age of 16. Shortly after settling
in New Zealand, he set up his first business as a painter and specialised coating contractor.

Following this, Trevor was instrumental in the foundation and development of a plastics company, which pioneered 'bubble' packag-
ing. As a result of the efforts and innovation of Trevor, his business
partner, and those he worked with, Conform Plastics Ltd received the
1978 Export award for their invention of bubble plastic mailing bags
and pool covers.

Shortly before their marriage in 1965 both Trevor and Jan experienced total transformation through Christian conversion. They became involved in a local church in Auckland where they served for the
next nineteen years.

In late 1985 Trevor and Jan were released to pursue their heart's
passion - evangelism, to see people motivated and trained in order to
see the nation of New Zealand impacted and transformed.

Trevor and Jan are committed to the training and development of
individuals, encouraging them to reach their full potential in order to
positively impact families and communities across New Zealand. They

endeavour to lead by example, serving God and people as they motivate, train and equip others to bring positive change into every sphere of our society.

Through the team they work with, they have seen the successful establishment of an evangelistic training centre known as Lifeway College, a community home for the disabled, a family-safe television station (Family Television Network), an international standard roller hockey rink for the local children, and the creation of a cartoon series committed to teaching positive values for children.

Thousands of people have been saved through the committed work of this couple, and many have been released through them into effective ministries.

They are passionate about family. Their first born Mark, born with Down's syndrome, is a continual delight to all around him. David was an up-and-coming evangelist, who at the age of sixteen and a half was killed in a tragic auto accident. In his last year, he led 80 young people to Christ, and was an example to all in his faith, integrity and enthusiasm. Rebecca, their gentle-hearted daughter has an incredible love and compassion for all around her. Married to David Price, they have produced two beautiful granddaughters who truly bring a sparkle to Trevor and Jan's eyes.

God will never be satisfied with a man
whose spiritual condition resembles a chimney sweep
covered with a white sheet.

WILLIAM BOOTH

Not only learn to use your weapons, and your armour,
and the rules of war, but how to put them into practice.
It is only by fighting that you will make warriors.

WILLIAM BOOTH

BOOTH
for today

REFLECTIONS by TREVOR YAXLEY

Hell No!

Booth once remonstrated: *"The chief danger of the 20th century will be religion without the Holy Ghost, Christianity without Christ, forgiveness without repentance, salvation without regeneration, politics without God, and Heaven without Hell."* Between the bookends of time, from Booth's day to this, it would seem that his statement is in many respects true.

However, I believe we have turned a corner and are now moving into a day the likes of which we have never seen before. The heartbeat of God is "intimacy with believers," and a "longing for souls." Karl Strader unfolds the true indicator of intimacy in the following statement: "The way I know I'm getting close to God: My heart begins to echo what His heart is saying - 'Souls, souls, souls!'"

There is a distinct parallel between Booth's time and our own. The landscape of the nations displays vividly our inability to handle human affairs with any level of success. We have once again hit an all time low. These are abnormal days and they require abnormal men and women with an inordinate appetite for self-sacrifice. Our world is now extremely vulnerable to the impact of passion filled prayer, and applied Christianity. God is once again raising an army as in William Booth's day. An army that will not have to whistle to keep up its courage, but one that is saturated with the presence, power and glory of God.

There are valuable lessons to be understood from the lives of both General Booth and his wife Catherine. The first is their all encompassing, motivating passion for the souls of men. Bramwell Booth writing on the tenth anniversary of his father's death stated: *"The overwhelming thing which impresses me concerning him is the way in which the need of his fellow-men had seized him. Their sins and miseries scorched him like flame."* [10]

Allow the words of Booth to challenge you today as they challenged countless men and women a century ago:

"What are you living for? What is the deep secret purpose that controls and fashions your existence? What do you eat and drink for? What is the end of your marrying and giving in marriage - your money-making and toilings and plannings? Is it the salvation of souls, the overthrow of the kingdom of evil and the setting up of the Kingdom of God? Have you the assurance that the ruling passion of your life is the same as that which brought Christ to the manger, led Him to fight the foul fiend of Hell in the wilderness, bore Him onward on the back of suffering and tears and ignominy and shame, sustained Him in drinking the cup of anguish and enduring the baptism of blood, bore Him through Gethsemane, nailed Him to the Cross of Calvary and enabled Him in triumph to open the gate of the Kingdom? Is this what you are living for? If not, you may be religious - a very proper person amongst religionists - but I don't see how you can be a Christian." [11]

Booth did not have a special gift or passion that any of us cannot have. He caught a vision of the heartbeat of the Father for the souls of men, for the lost, then proceded to do something about it. We too can catch the Father's heartbeat for souls and follow William Booth's example of action.

"For God so loved the world that He gave His one and only Son, that whoever believes in Him shall not perish, but have eternal life." JOHN 3:16

If God was willing to give that much, we too should be willing to lay down our lives for our fellow man.

"Everyone who calls on the name of the Lord will be saved. How, then, can they call on the one they have not believed in? And how can they believe in the one of whom they have not heard? And how can they hear without someone preaching to them? And how can they preach unless they are sent?" ROMANS 10:13-15

Preaching or sharing the good news of the gospel is not the domain of the few anointed with the preaching gift. It is the privilege we all have. God can use you in your own unique way, to share how you have made His wonderful gift of salvation your own.

"Go into all the world and preach the good news to all creation." MARK 16:15

Here is our commissioning and sending. There are no exceptions - every Christian is commanded to go!

> *"This is good and pleases God our Saviour, who wants all men*
> *to be saved and to come to a knowledge of the truth."*
> 1 TIMOTHY 2:3-4

What a wonderful privilege to know that the God of the universe can use you to be His agent to bring the message of hope and good news to people. The result for them will be eternal life instead of eternal damnation and torment in the fires of hell.

Excessive Obedience

Obedience is one of those words with negative connotations when used in our daily conversation. Our cultural Christianity has taught us that all we need do is listen to God, and as long as we acknowledge the Word of God as correct all will be well with our soul.

Booth displayed a different character quality; he heard and obeyed. His practical application of God's Word translated to everyday life brought about great blessing to the destitute of his day and to the heart of God.

We all desire to live a successful life and fulfil the destiny that God has marked out for us, but this will not be possible without excessive obedience.

General Booth was quick to obey the divine strategies given him. Procrastination was not a trait he cherished but one he disdained. He hated to waste time. When he travelled he arranged brief meetings to make good use of transit times between trains, and he made use of every opportunity with people of influence to further the cause of the Army. Booth's aim was always to use every moment to its utmost. He loathed carelessness, indifference and half-heartedness. Through prompt action and attention to detail he utilised his God-given gifts and achieved the seemingly impossible.

One day we will face the Lord as Booth has, and He will say, "I gave you a gift, what did you do with it?" What will we say? Nothing... It will be too late! I trust He will not be able to say, "I placed in you My Spirit. I gave you My authority, My power, My strength, My virtue, My compassion, My grace, My love, My name, My presence, My anointing. You could have changed your community, impacted your nation and influenced the world. But, you chose to watch television instead!!!"

Let us not neglect the gift God has placed within us, but with a "hot pursuit," track hard after obedience. He will require a return on His investment. Our actions will need to speak louder than our words on "that day." It is never enough to hear the call of God. We must become people who "Just do it."

The time for looking on, singing about, debating over and discussing the problem of sin and the cure of the cross is over. It is time to rise and fight!

William Booth took seriously the command of his Commander in Chief. Jesus said, "Go," so he just did it! His response was raw obedience, blind faith and an absolute commitment to the divine command. God's command is the same to us today.

> *"Go into all the world and preach the good news to all creation. Whoever believes and is baptised will be saved, but whoever does not believe will be condemned. And these signs will accompany those who believe: In my name they will drive out demons; they will speak in new tongues; they will pick up snakes with their hands; and when they drink deadly poison, it will not hurt them at all; they will place their hands on sick people, and they will get well."* MARK 16:15-18

This command, when obeyed, goes far beyond selfishly looking for our own blessing. It brings great blessing to others in the form of eternal life, freedom, speaking in new tongues, divine protection and divine healing.

Obedience and blessing go hand in hand - you will be blessed as you obey, but the recipients of your obedience will be blessed even more.

> *"Now if you obey me fully and keep my covenant, then out of all the nations you will be my treasured possession. Although the whole earth is mine, you will be for me a kingdom of priests and a holy nation."* EXODUS 19:5-6[A]

Think of your most treasured possession. Now consider the width and breadth of the world. God, who created all things, knows and sees your obedience and desire to be a "covenant keeper," because His eye scans the earth constantly. Your obedience puts you in God's "treasure box" and selects you, out of the whole earth, as a priest unto God.

> *"Does the Lord delight in burnt offerings and sacrifices as much as in obeying the voice of the Lord? To obey is better than sacrifice, and to heed is better than fat of rams."* 1 SAMUEL 15:22

Consider these words of Scripture: "to obey is better than sacrifice." All we do that is not the result of an obedient heart responding out of love for God is empty ritual; lifeless religion. Sacrifice is essential in the life of a believer, however if the sacrifice is not made out of obedience to God because of our love for Him, we are missing the point. Our heart motives are of prime importance to God.

There is no way around it, the blessing of obedience cannot be bought, begged or borrowed. Even though obedience may be costly, excessive obedience always results in excessive blessing.

Innovate & Initiate

Mediocrity lulls us into an attitude of sitting back and 'wowing' the efforts of others that hit the mark and make a difference. It has been said that spectators eventually become critics and this state of criticism or jealousy can squash the potential to be world-changers.

Everything we use, enjoy or find convenient has had some innovator and initiator. For many of these people the cost was great. They were undermined and ridiculed by the jealousy and criticism of people happy with mediocrity. Imagine if the inventors of the motorcar or the flush toilet gave in to the temptation to sit back and take it easy.

Within each one of us is the potential to be innovators and initiators - all it requires is the realisation of the wonderfully creative resources available for us to tap into. We need to take the blindfolds off our eyes and simply see the need. We can be part of the answer! The Creator of the universe lives within every Christian and He gives wonderfully individual solutions to each and every lack.

Time and again, William Booth saw a need, a possibility and a challenge. Again and again he stepped outside the constraints of the day and found unorthodox remedies to each situation of need. This resulted in the wonderful work of the Salvation Army, a work known and respected throughout the world today.

Such was the courage of this man, that no barriers were insurmountable or immovable. What a challenge to us today!

There were no "if only's" in his vocabulary; just a raw determination, spirited creativity and trust in the relationships of respected people around him. He saw a need, dreamed a dream and together they saw it through to the end because William Booth knew he was in partnership with the Creator.

"In the beginning God created the heavens and the earth."
GENESIS 1:1

The creation story described in Genesis is the first and most dramatic record of the work of our initiating, innovating Creator. With unlimited creative power, God formed from nothing, the universe and everything in it! When God stood back to assess His handiwork, His comment on all he had created was that "it was good." God took great delight and satisfaction in all he made.

History too is full of many examples of godly people who "stepped out of the box" and partnered with God to perform mighty works. These history makers employed creative thinking, drawing on their God-given gifts and the creative power of the Spirit within them to accomplish great works for God.

"You shall receive power when the Holy Spirit comes on you; and you will be my witnesses ..." ACTS 1:8

William Booth co-operated with the Holy Spirit to implement creative solutions to the needs around him. This same power is available to us today not just to speak, but also to do the works of God.

When Peter, newly filled with the Holy Spirit, stood up to address the crowd, he was a transformed man. Acts 2:14-41 gives us a glimpse of a man of power and authority who stood as spokesman for the disciples. It was only a few short weeks earlier that he, as a stammering deserter, denied his relationship with Jesus three times. Now, as he encountered the power of the Holy Spirit, he stood in a public place, condemned the people for crucifying Jesus and began declaring their need for repentance and baptism. The result - some three thousand were added to the church that day. What an example of working hand in hand with the Creator. Peter was able to do something quite outside of his natural talents and ability as he was obedient to the leading of the Holy Spirit. The same Holy Spirit empowers us as believers today.

"He is able to do exceedingly abundantly above all that we ask or think, according to the power that works in us."
EPHESIANS 3:20

As we unite and co-operate with the Holy Spirit, we will be delighted to see this Scripture come about before our very eyes! Remember, it is His power in us that makes the difference.

High Cost

The cost of true Christianity today is no different from the early days of The Salvation Army. The demands of the Gospel made by

Jesus are still applicable to all that take upon themselves the name of Christ. We stumble over the twin truths that salvation is a gift, yet the cost to those who receive it is "everything."

To most of us, it would appear Booth paid a high price. Persecution came from every angle. His life seemed to perpetually invite hardship to his side. *"We must have gotten hold of something good,"* he once stated, *"because Hell is so evidently excited about it."* Later he exclaimed, *"We must be right! Who can question it when this is the sort of opposition we meet with?"* There is no doubt about it - he and Catherine had obtained a significant reputation...in Hell!!!

These warriors of the nineteenth century had learned that as followers of Jesus they must deny themselves, consider themselves dead, lay aside all selfish ambitions and take up their cross.

The cross to the General represented the death of all that he held near and dear to him. Like the first century believers, it meant much more than the thought of long-term problems and difficulties, although they were consistently present. On the contrary, Booth knew the cross was the cruel instrument of torture that would bring him to his death in the most agonising way known to mankind. William Booth understood that he was called by God to die.

To many, it seems too high a price to pay, and yet compared to the riches of Christ we receive as believers, it is nothing. John MacArthur described this level of commitment well:

"This is the kind of totally committed response the Lord Jesus called for. A desire for Him at any cost. Absolute surrender. A full exchange of self for the Saviour. It is the only response that will open the gates of the Kingdom. Seen through the eyes of this world, it is as high a price as anyone can pay. But from a kingdom perspective, it is really no sacrifice at all." [6]

The most valuable things in life usually have the highest cost. There is nothing more valuable on earth, nor more costly, than intimacy with the King of Kings - being under His command and having His ear.

"I press on toward the goal to win the prize for which God has called me heavenward in Christ Jesus." PHILIPPIANS 3:14

There will be countless things to entice you from the goal - many of which are not considered 'bad.' Athletes training for their 'big event' sacrifice social life, favourite foods and they beat their bodies into submission as the price of attaining the prize which is but a fleeting moment of glory.

We must do the same with ourselves as we walk in obedience to the Lord Jesus Christ. This is the day for focus. You cannot be focused on more than one thing at a time. Our natural eyes are made for single focus - so are our spiritual eyes. If we are focused on the King of Kings, no price will be too high, no cost too great to pay for Him.

"And he died for all, that those who live should no longer live for themselves but for him who died for them and was raised again." 2 CORINTHIANS 5:15

"You are not your own; you were bought at a price."
1 CORINTHIANS 6:19^B-20^A

Each of us was purchased at the greatest possible price - the life of Jesus, the Son of God. The truth is, our lives are not our own; we belong to God. William Booth was prepared to pay the price of his own life for the sake of the call. Take time now to sincerely ask the Holy Spirit to help you examine your own heart and determine the cost you are willing to pay in your call to serve Christ.

"But whatever was to my profit I now consider loss for the sake of Christ. What is more, I consider everything a loss compared to the surpassing greatness of knowing Christ Jesus my Lord, for whose sake I have lost all things. I consider them rubbish, that I may obtain Christ..." PHILIPPIANS 3:7-8

Who said this? Paul of Tarsus - the most respected, most educated nobleman of the near east. His influence and potential were unsurpassed. Yet he was prepared to rubbish it all for the privilege of following and serving Christ.

Are you prepared to follow Jesus, no matter what it will cost you?

To Gain, Train

Booth understood that life is for training and training is for life. He submitted his own life to be trained according to the Word of God. He learned early in his journey to glean all he could from the great men and women of God in his time.

As disciples of Christ, we all undergo a lifetime of personal training. A disciple is not just a student receiving information, but an apprentice, one who learns to model their life after the life of their Teacher.

We must be prepared to train hard, to accept the instruction of the Word of God and the 'fathers' of the faith, applying it diligently to our lives. The race we run is not a hundred metre sprint, it's a marathon. Like Booth, with our focus clearly on the goal, we must choose to train well and run to win. Each of us is responsible for our own preparation and training. We are also responsible to prepare and train others.

I have heard it said, "Success without a successor is failure." How true.

Some years ago I had the opportunity to spend time with a dear friend. He had ministered around the world for the best part of his life. God anointed him powerfully, with many signs and wonders following his preaching of the Word. As we walked in the park that day he was overcome with a sense of deep disappointment. His heart poured out its grief, "If only I had trained other young ministers; if only I had taken them with me on my trips. At the time it just seemed like too much bother to be worth it. Now my time is coming to an end and I have no one to carry on the work God gave me to do." He died a short time later!

Not so with General William Booth; a salute is in order in this regard. Rarely was there an opportunity missed for "on the job training" of others. Army stories say that Booth preached some of his best sermons through the lips of other men - often through illiterate men. "He never monopolised the meetings. He made others help him - they were as much theirs, as his." The involvement of new converts in the work of the gospel encouraged both them and the Army to grow.

Booth organised his people and provided a place for each of them. He was determined even the newest recruit would feel he or she was making a meaningful contribution to the advancement of the gospel. "I want you all in the thick of the battle; remember victory or defeat depends on your own particular bayonet point," was repeatedly his strong encouragement.

We learn from Booth the longevity and success of any work of God is found in the number of those we have trained. Achievement may be measured by looking at those who are on the field doing the job far more productively than we could ever have done alone.

"Come, follow me," Jesus said, "and I will make you fishers of men." MATTHEW 4:19

Jesus' first simple words to Simon and Peter were the beginning of the most wonderful traineeship ever undertaken on earth. These words bore the challenge to leave family, fortune and familiarity and to become the first to carry on the ministry of Jesus Christ when He departed to His heavenly home three years later.

As they journeyed together Jesus taught his disciples in three stages:

Stage 1: Jesus did the works and the disciples watched

Stage 2: The disciples did the works and Jesus watched

Stage 3: Jesus ascended to heaven and the disciples, empowered by the Spirit, put into practice all they had learned

What a wonderful example of training and discipleship given to us by Jesus.

"Therefore I urge you to imitate me. For this reason I am sending to you Timothy, my son whom I love, who is faithful in the Lord. He will remind you of my way of life in Christ Jesus, which agrees with what I teach everywhere in every church." 1 CORINTHIANS 4:16-18

"If Timothy comes, see to it that he has nothing to fear while he is with you, for he is carrying on the work of the Lord, just as I am. No one, then, should refuse to accept him."
1 CORINTHIANS 16:10-11[A]

Paul's life was an example worthy of imitating - his lifestyle and ministry lined up with what he taught. He had confidence that Timothy would carry on the work of the Lord according to his own model of ministry. He knew the work would be done well. Timothy's training and discipleship under Paul meant the people would accept Timothy and the message of the gospel.

Regardless of our own stage of development and ministry, there are always others hungry to grow, learn and receive an impartation of what God has given and taught us. It is vital that our lives, like Paul, are an example, which can be safely followed.

A Broken Heart

Hellish sounds, sights and smells can either repulse us and cause us to turn away, or we can allow God to use them to touch the depths of our hearts with the softening of His Spirit. God can use the haunting memories of past pain to etch compassion deep within us for those unable to escape their personal hell by their own efforts. We choose daily either to allow or disallow what we see, feel and sense around us to stir compassion in our hearts in response to overwhelming need.

William Booth took hold of every opportunity to reach out with more than a "hand out," but a "hand up" to those miserable souls caught in unending and heart rending situations.

The challenge to do the same today has not changed. Although the type of situations facing us may vary from those faced by Booth, the nature of the need remains the same. Circumstances still crush the spirit and soul and break the hearts of men, women and children around us in this post-modern society.

The answer to every need is timeless: the hand of Jesus extended in love, compassion, practical assistance and the gospel of salvation to breathe life into lifeless souls.

William Booth watched his work grow from the humble beginnings of providing Christmas dinners, to encompass soup kitchens, refuge homes, shelters, a farm colony, missing persons bureau, legal aid service brokeries and a poor mans bank. As we begin to reach out to one person at a time, the economy of God will ensure that even the most humble efforts are multiplied with His grace and provision to ensure significant results.

You may personally have been rescued from awful poverty, either naturally or spiritually. You may know what it is to suffer the pain of abuse, grief, sickness or poverty. You and I now have the awesome privilege of using our own experience of deliverance and healing to bring relief and salvation to countless suffering souls.

Let the example of William Booth's broken heart for the lost spur us on to greater measures of love and compassion; measures that God will take and multiply for the extension of His kingdom.

> *"The Spirit of the Sovereign Lord is on me, because the Lord has anointed me to preach good news to the poor. He has sent me to bind up the broken-hearted, to proclaim freedom for the captives and release from darkness for the prisoners, to proclaim the year of the Lord's favour and the day of vengeance of our God, to comfort all who mourn, and provide for those who grieve in Zion - to bestow on them a crown of beauty instead of ashes, the oil of gladness instead of mourning, and a garment of praise instead of a spirit of despair."* ISAIAH 61:1-3

This scripture is full of promise, possibility and challenge for each and every Christian. It is not just for ministers, pastors and leaders, but also for all who know Christ. It is the essence of the ministry of Jesus to a hurting world through every believer.

> *"Go therefore, and teach all nations, baptising them in the name of the Father, and of the Son, and of the Holy Spirit."*
> MATTHEW 28:19

The Great Commission is a command that is backed up with the promise of Isaiah 61. The Holy Spirit is given for the empowerment of believers to do all that Christ commands. When Jesus left this earth and rose to join His Father in heaven, he told the disciples that He would send a comforter and helper - The Holy Spirit. This third Person of the Godhead is resident within us to be our helper as we obey what Jesus has asked us to do. He is just a heartbeat, a quiet breathed prayer away, waiting for us to call on Him for the help and power we so desperately need.

"I can do everything through Him who gives me strength."
PHILIPPIANS 4:13

With the magnitude of spiritual and natural poverty around us, it is easy to become overwhelmed and discouraged. Yet, nothing surprises God. When your heart breaks under the weight of the needs around you, God's strength will flow in coupled with His compassion and you will achieve great things for Him. As you slip your hand in His, desiring to obey His command to "Go," and by faith believing that the Spirit of the Sovereign Lord empowers you to do His works, you will be delighted and amazed at how He will take your efforts and work mightily, even though you may feel they are unrefined and immature.

Prayer, Faith and the Power of the Spirit

Throughout history, men and women have sought success in politics, riches, fame and religion. The eyes of the world are often focused on the 'successful,' but only the outward signs are seen. It is God who sees and knows the heart of man and unless the success is born of God it is merely 'skin deep.'

Success which is born of God is conceived by the Spirit and brought forth by the Spirit's power into reality. Faith is a key ingredient as we labour in persistent, prevailing prayer to see the purposes of the heart of God come into being.

Imagine the ridiculous sight of someone with a big umbrella in a group of people praying for rain - when they were in the midst of a major drought! This is faith in action. He would have been ridiculed and mocked and endured a real test of his faith. Persecution thwarts the puny; his faith-filled action proved his stature. He was not intimidated.

Faith, prayer and the power of the Spirit are inseparable. Prayer and power are inseparable. Paul's exhortation to Timothy to pray with supplications, prayers, intercessions and thanks, still challenges us. Prayer is the domain of all believers - sadly, we relegate it to the few.

It is necessary to exert yourself in prayer. We exert ourselves in the pursuit of financial gain, popularity, influence and sporting achievements. It is far more beneficial to strive in the arena of prayer to achieve eternal gains.

We have an enemy who is named as the "prince of the power of the air." He is a powerful force in this world, working against everything God has ordained. The victory of Calvary has to be enforced against him and this victory will only be achieved by faith-filled, prevailing prayer. He will relinquish nothing except that which is taken from him by prayer, impassioned and inspired by the Holy Spirit. William Booth's example is worthy of following - give yourself to prayer, put aside everything that hinders the work of the Spirit in and through your life and the exceptional results that Booth witnessed will be yours. We like Booth must remember:

> *"The Holy Ghost convicting people of sin, making them saints and soldiers - sacrificing, weeping, toiling to save men from sin and hell - there is our power in a nutshell."* [9]

> *"He replied, "Because you have so little faith. I tell you the truth, if you have faith as small as a mustard seed, you can say to this mountain, 'Move from here to there,' and it will move. Nothing will be impossible for you."* MATTHEW 17:20

Although the disciples had been with Jesus for years, they still had little faith. Jesus encourages them, assuring them that even the smallest amount of faith will do the greatest works. No matter how small your faith is, even as small as the tiniest seed on earth, if you employ it to do the works of Jesus, results equal to the moving of mountains will be yours.

> *"Therefore I tell you, whatever you ask for in prayer, believe that you have received it, and it will be yours."* MARK 11:24

Prayer and faith are inseparable. Every prayer must be charged with faith. If not, it is little more than hot air. Tremendous frustration is the result of unanswered prayer. The key is faith, which in itself is available only from God as a gift. Ask Him today for this gift - He will not disappoint you.

"We live by faith, not by sight." 2 CORINTHIANS 5:7

Faith is not faith unless we know we have something as yet unseen. This is the essence of the Christian life.

"Now faith is being sure of what we hope for and certain of what we do not see." HEBREWS 11:1

The giants of faith mentioned in Hebrews 11 exercised faith through sacrifice, righteousness, pleasing God, building an ark, obedience, re-locating homes, overcoming physical impossibility to become a father and much more. As you study the examples of these lives, allow them to build your faith. May the power of the Spirit come upon your faith-filled prayer and enable you to do works as awesome as these.

Finishing the Race

Life can be compared to a steeplechase relay, with its ups and downs, water jumps and difficult patches alongside clear straights where the running is easy. We have all seen runners at the beginning of an important race - every muscle tensed, eyes fixed on the track ahead, alert with every cell attentive. With incredible anticipation they wait for the firing of the shot that heralds the beginning of the race for which they have diligently trained.

It is crucial to begin each race with the intention of finishing one's own part of the relay and to pass the baton on without fumbling. Relays have been won or lost entirely because of the ease or difficulty in passing the baton at the change point.

If one runner decides they are too tired or they don't like the course, the whole race would be in vain for the rest of the team. It is just as important to finish well, as it is to begin well!

William Booth knew this principle, and used it when training others to carry on the work he had begun. Even in his later years, with failing eyesight and health, he worked diligently with his customary zeal. This zeal, which is defined as fervent devotion, transcends the limitations of age, disability or gender.

It is the zeal of the Lord that will inspire you to reach out to just one more lost soul when your own soul is flagging. This zeal is the quality that makes the elderly, fiery servants of the Lord or the disabled, able to be effective in their own individual races.

No matter what baton you hold, now is the time to ensure that others are trained and prepared to receive it from you. There is nothing that you are doing for the Lord that is unworthy of being passed on to another when your race is over. We may estimate that our days are 'three score years and ten,' but history proves this is not always the case. Some of God's choicest saints have lived very short lives.

Now is the time to search out the next generation baton carriers. Now is the time to pour into them the full sum of the wealth God has poured into you.

All through the Bible we see a pattern for our lives, an example for us to follow. As Jesus was resurrected and left this earth for His heavenly home He delivered the 'Great Commission' to us. This in essence was his 'passing of the baton.' He had run the race, run it perfectly, and this was the time for Him to pass the responsibility of carrying on His work to us.

"I consider my life worth nothing to me, if only I may finish the race and complete the task the Lord Jesus has given me - the task of testifying to the gospel of God's grace." ACTS 20:24

As Paul farewelled the elders of the Ephesian church with these words, he had the finish line clearly in sight. The purpose of his life is defined by his all-consuming passion to spread the gospel. Nothing else mattered. To Paul, his life journey was like a race. He knew that only those who run well, those who press through with persistence and perseverance, reach their goal.

"I press on toward the goal to win the prize for which God has called me heavenward in Christ Jesus." PHILIPPIANS 3:14

Toward the end of his life, Paul was able to look back and declare that he had fought the good fight. His service for God had been a fight - a fight to keep his feet from stumbling; a fight to keep his determination strong; a fight to keep his eyes on the finish line. The life of every believer is not only a race, but also a fight. Jesus is the author and finisher of our faith. With Him we can run any race and fight the good fight of faith, no matter how difficult it gets.

"I have fought the good fight, I have finished the race, I have kept the faith." 2 TIMOTHY 4:7

Paul placed great importance on mentoring Timothy. Together they experienced good times and bad. As Paul's own life came to a close, he was able to 'pass the baton' on to the one who had run the race with him.

This is our example; there are many Timothy's waiting with hands extended for the baton of the future. Don't leave them empty-handed. Place your baton in these willing hands and marvel at how God will multiply all that He has taught you.

Who Cares?

The vision God gave William Booth inspired and energised him to a lifetime of selfless labour in the rescue of lost souls.

As he saw the teeming multitude drowning while so many went blindly about their duties, past-times and religious practice, his heart turned toward the lost, never to turn back again. Booth was spurred on, even until his last breath, with this vision constantly before him, having been etched into the very fibre of his being.

In this day, the Spirit of God is beckoning and imploring each and every believer to co-labour with Christ in the rescue of those in our world who are perishing spiritually, just as surely as the drowning masses in Booth's vision. The ongoing tragedy is that few hear and even fewer heed this call.

William Booth is a wonderful example of what God can do with just one life; a life of little education, means or great natural talent. Booth could easily have looked upon the little he had and justifiably disqualified himself. Instead, he chose to look at the might, power and provision of God. Booth was a man who firmly believed that even one man plus God was a majority!

He did all he could to obey God. The results of his obedience are outstanding. His efforts, vision and courage powerfully impacted the

British Isles and his influence is still evident throughout much of the world today.

Do you hear the impassioned plea of the Spirit of God to join with Him, even as William Booth did, to see souls snatched from the fire of eternal damnation and gloriously saved? Will you join the ranks of the great army God is raising up for these last days?
The challenge is before you; the choice is yours. What will you do?

Leonard Ravenhill once penned:

A vision without a task makes a visionary;

A task without a vision makes for drudgery;

A task wedded to a vision makes a missionary.

"Write down the vision and make it plain on tablets so that he may run who reads it." HABAKKUK 2:2

Scripture challenges us to live life with purpose and clear direction. We need a clear vision to keep us focussed through the challenges and disappointments of life. Booth's burden for the lost and his God-given strategy to bring them into the kingdom, directed him to a life of divine passion and clear purpose.

"Cherish your visions and your dreams as they are the children of your soul; the blueprints of your ultimate achievements." NAPOLEON HILL

A life of significance is one invested in people for the purpose of furthering God's Kingdom. Such a life will be remembered far beyond the grave, as others captivated and inspired by the vision carry on the work. Selfish ambition and desire dies with the person, but the love of God outworked, spans generations.

"Where there is no vision the people perish." PROVERBS 29:18

In other versions of this Scripture, it states that without revelation, people cast off restraint and live carelessly, without purpose. Careless Christianity is affecting this present generation. Many lack the purpose and discipline of generations past in strategically impacting our communities, cities and nations with the gospel.

Put your vision and desire on paper today, and ask God to ignite a growing hunger within you to significantly impact those around you.

May God so pour His passion into your heart that rest will not come until the mandate of your calling to this generation has been fulfilled.

REFERENCES

CHAPTER ONE • HELL NO!

1. Jenty Fairbank, *William and Catherine Booth*: God's soldiers (London: Hodder and Stoughton, 1974), 30.
2. Edward Bishop, *Blood and Fire* (London: Longmans, 1964), 19.
3. Cyril Barnes, *Words of Catherine Booth* (London: Salvationist Publishing and Supplies, 1981), 9.
4. John Coutts, *The Booths' American Mentors* (Issue 26, 1990), 22.
5. Catherine Bramwell-Booth, *Catherine Booth* (London: Hodder and Stoughton, 1970), 198.
6. General Bramwell Booth, *Our First Captain* (London: Salvationist Publishing).
7. Richard Collier, *The General Next to God* (London: Collins, 1965), 46.
8. Richard Collier, *The General Next to God* (London: Collins, 1965), 53.
9. William Booth, *The Salvationist*, Jan 1879 quoted in *The Founder Speaks Again* (London: Salvationist Publishing and Supplies, 1960), 45-48.
10. General Bramwell Booth, *Our First Captain* (London: Salvationist Publishing and Supplies), 5.
11. General William Booth, *The War Cry*, Feb 21 1885 quoted in *The Founder Speaks Again* (London: Salvationist Publishing and Supplies, 1960), 60.

CHAPTER TWO • EXCESSIVE OBEDIENCE

1. Catherine Bramwell-Booth, *Catherine Booth* (London: Hodder and Stoughton, 1970), 233.
2. Edward Bishop, *Blood and Fire* (London: Longmans, 1964), 44.
3. Richard Collier, *The General Next to God* (London: Collins, 1965), 56.

4.   General Bramwell Booth, *Our First Captain* (London: Salvationist Publishing and Supplies), 17.

5.   General William Booth, *The War Cry*, Jan 20 1881 quoted in *The Founder Speaks Again* (London: Salvationist Publishing and Supplies, 1960), 100.

6.   General William Booth, *The War Cry*, Jan 20 1881 quoted in *The Founder Speaks Again* (London: Salvationist Publishing and Supplies, 1960), 100.

7.   General William Booth, *A New Year's Eve Greeting*, 1906 quoted in *The Founder Speaks Again* (London: Salvationist Publishing and Supplies, 1960), 162.

8.   E.M. Bounds, *The Complete Works of E.M. Bounds on Prayer* (Grand Rapids: Baker Books, 1990), 104.

9.   Richard Collier, *The General Next to God* (London: Collins, 1965), 210.

CHAPTER THREE • INNOVATE AND INITIATE

1.   Catherine Bramwell-Booth, *Catherine Booth* (London: Hodder and Stoughton, 1970), 119.

2.   Catherine Bramwell-Booth, *Catherine Booth* (London: Hodder and Stoughton, 1970), 122.

3.   General Frederick Coutts, *No Discharge in This War* (London: Hodder and Stoughton, 1974), 27.

4.   Cyril Barnes, *Words of Catherine Booth* (London: Salvationist Publishing and Supplies, 1981), 19.

5.   Richard Collier, *The General Next to God* (London: Collins, 1965), 41.

6.   Richard Collier, *The General Next to God* (London: Collins, 1965), 70.

7.   General William Booth, *The East London Evangelist Dec 1868* quoted in *The Founder Speaks Again* (London: Salvationist Publishing and Supplies, 1960), 57.

CHAPTER FOUR • HIGH COST

1.   Richard Collier, *The General Next to God* (London: Collins, 1965), 106.

2.   General William Booth, *The Seven Spirits* (London: The Salvation Army, 1985), 91.

3.   General Bramwell Booth, *Our First Captain* (London: Salvationist Publishing and Supplies) 16.

4.   Richard Collier, *The General Next to God* (London: Collins, 1965), 90.

5.   General William Booth, *The War Cry*, May 23, 1885 quoted in *The Founder Speaks Again* (London: Salvationist Publishing and Supplies, 1960), 175.

6.   John F. MacArthur, Jr, *The Gospel According to Jesus* (Grand Rapids: Zondervan Publishing House, 1988), 141.

CHAPTER FIVE • TO GAIN, TRAIN

1.   Richard Collier, *The General Next to God* (London: Collins, 1965), 146.

2.   General William Booth, *Eightieth Birthday Letter* quoted in *The Founder Speaks Again* (London: Salvationist Publishing And Supplies, 1960), 168.

3.   General William Booth, *A New Year's Greeting 1906* quoted in *The Founder Speaks Again* (London: Salvationist Publishing and Supplies, 1960), 163.

4.   Richard Collier, *The General Next to God* (London: Collins, 1965), 57.

5.   Jenty Fairbank, *William and Catherine Booth: God's soldiers* (London: Hodder and Stoughton, 1974), 101.

6.   Catherine Bramwell-Booth, *Catherine Booth* (London: Hodder and Stoughton, 1970), 209.

7.   Catherine Bramwell-Booth, *Catherine Booth* (London: Hodder and Stoughton, 1970), 243.

8.   Catherine Bramwell-Booth, *Catherine Booth* (London: Hodder and Stoughton, 1970), 219.

9.   Catherine Bramwell-Booth, *Catherine Booth* (London: Hodder and Stoughton, 1970), 252.

10.   Richard Collier, *The General Next to God* (London: Collins, 1965), 89.

11.   Richard Collier, *The General Next to God* (London: Collins, 1965), 179.

12.   Jenty Fairbank, *William and Catherine Booth: God's soldiers* (London: Hodder and Stoughton, 1974), 82, 85.

13.   General William Booth, *The Salvationist, Nov 1879* quoted in *The Founder Speaks Again* (London: Salvationist Publishing and Supplies, 1960), 54.

14.   General Bramwell Booth, *Our First Captain* (London: Salvationist Publishing and Supplies), 10.

CHAPTER SIX • A BROKEN HEART

1.   Richard Collier, *The General Next to God* (London: Collins, 1965), 58.

2.   Jenty Fairbank, *William and Catherine Booth: God's soldiers* (London: Hodder and Stoughton, 1974), 72-73.

3.   Richard Collier, *The General Next to God* (London: Collins, 1965), 175.

4.   General William Booth, *In Darkest England And The Way Out*, quoted in *The Founder Speaks Again* (London: Salvationist Publishing and Supplies, 1960), 155.

5.   Richard Collier, *The General Next to God* (London: Collins, 1965), 188.

6.   Richard Collier, *The General Next to God* (London: Collins, 1965), 188.

7.   Richard Collier, *The General Next to God* (London: Collins, 1965), 190.

8.   General William Booth, *In Darkest England And The Way Out* (London: The Salvation Army, 1890), Dedication.

9.   Harold Begbie, *Life of William Booth - The Founder of the Salvation Army* (London: McMillan & Co, 1920), vol 1, 375.

10.   Richard Collier, *The General Next to God* (London: Collins, 1965), 194

CHAPTER SEVEN • PRAYER, FAITH AND THE POWER OF THE SPIRIT

1.   General William Booth, *The Christian Mission Magazine Jan 1870* quoted in *The Founder Speaks Again* (London: Salvationist Publishing and Supplies, 1960), 71.

2.   General William Booth, *New Year's Address 1906* quoted in *The Founder Speaks Again* (London: Salvationist Publishing and Supplies, 1960), 163.

3.   General William Booth, *The Christian Mission Magazine Jan 1870* quoted in *The Founder Speaks Again* (London: Salvationist Publishing and Supplies, 1960), 76.

4.   Leonard Ravenhill, *Why Revival Tarries* (Minneapolis: Bethany House Publishers, 1959), 51.

5.   Richard Collier, *The General Next to God* (London: Collins, 1965), 222-223.

6.   General William Booth, *New Year's Address 1906* quoted in *The Founder Speaks Again* (London: Salvationist Publishing and Supplies, 1960), 165.

7.   Catherine Bramwell-Booth, *Catherine Booth* (London: Hodder and Stoughton, 1970), 246.

8.   Catherine Bramwell-Booth, *Catherine Booth* (London: Hodder and Stoughton, 1970), 240.

9.   Harold Begbie, *Life of William Booth - The Founder of The Salvation Army* (London: McMillan & Co, 1920), Vol 2, 180.

CHAPTER EIGHT • FINISHING THE RACE

1.   General Frederick Coutts, *No Discharge in This War* (London: Hodder and Stoughton, 1974), 139.

2.   J. Evan Smith, *Booth The Beloved - Personal Recollection of William Booth, Founder of The Salvation Army* (London: Oxford University Press, 1949), 38.

3.   General William Booth, *The Last Public Address May 9, 1912* quoted in *The Founder Speaks Again* (London: Salvationist Publishing and Supplies, 1960), 169-170.

4.   Richard Collier, *The General Next to God* (London: Collins, 1965), 247.

CHAPTER NINE • WHO CARES?

1.   General William Booth, *Who Cares?* from The War Cry, June 20, 1912 quoted in *The Founder Speaks Again* (London: Salvationist Publishing and Supplies, 1960), 61-67.

BIBLIOGRAPHY

General Frederick Coutts, *No Discharge in This War* (London: Hodder and Stoughton, 1974)

Richard Collier, *The General Next to God* (London: Collins, 1965)

Catherine Bramwell-Booth, *Catherine Booth* (London: Hodder and Stoughton, 1970)

General William Booth, *Assorted Writings* quoted in *The Founder Speaks Again* (London: Salvationist Publishing and Supplies, 1960)

Cyril Barnes, *Words of Catherine Booth* (London: Salvationist Publishing and Supplies, 1981)

Harold Begbie, *Life of William Booth - The Founder of the Salvation Army* (London: McMillan & Co, 1920) Vol 1&2.

General William Booth, *In Darkest England And The Way Out* (London: The Salvation Army, 1890)

Jenty Fairbank, *William and Catherine Booth: God's soldiers* (London: Hodder and Stoughton, 1974)

Cyril Barnes, *Words of Catherine Booth* (London: Salvationist Publishing and Supplies, 1981)

General Bramwell Booth, *Our First Captain* (London: Salvationist Publishing)

General William Booth, *The Seven Spirits* (London: The Salvation Army, 1985)

Edward Bishop, *Blood and Fire* (London: Longmans, 1964)

J. Evan Smith, *Booth the Beloved - Personal Recollection of William Booth, Founder of The Salvation Army* (London: Oxford University Press, 1949)

Army 100 First Wave

"So I prophesied as he commanded me, and breath came unto them and they stood upon their feet, an exceedingly great army" EZEKIEL 37:10

The time is now, Wesley in his day stated:

"Give me 100 preachers who hate nothing but sin and love nothing but God and I care not a straw whether they be clergy or laymen, such alone will shake the gates of hell and set up the kingdom of Heaven on earth. God does nothing but in answer to prayer." JOHN WESLEY

Many of us have waited for the appointed time when God's Spirit would impact New Zealand and the nations. These days of waiting are over.

In direct response to this challenge, five and a half months intensive specialised training will commence at Lifeway College, North Auckland, New Zealand from March 2000.

People who rise to the challenge will be part of the 100 First Wave Army, carrying a passion for God and fiery love for souls launching them into disciplined, concentrated effort to bring change in the nations.

Working alongside local churches, the army will start from all four corners of New Zealand and sweep through every town and city, sharing their faith, praying for the sick, and mobilising the saints to action. Once this work is sufficiently underway, the army will launch to the nations fulfilling New Zealand's calling as a missionary sending people.

Is this God's destiny for your life?

Contact us for more information and a free prospectus:

Trevor & Jan Yaxley,
100 First Wave Army
Lifeway Trust Inc.,
PO Box 303, Warkworth,
New Zealand.
Phone: +64-9-425 4054
Fax: +64-9-425 4053
Email: tybusiness@maxnet.co.nz

"He is no fool who gives up what he cannot keep in order to gain what he cannot lose."

JIM ELLIOT *martyred missionary to the Auca Indians*